Cook-A-Book

Reading Activities for Grades Pre-K to 6

2nd Edition

Leslie Cefali

Alleyside Press

Fort Atkinson, Wisconsin

Published by Alleyside Press,
an imprint of Highsmith Press LLC
Highsmith Press
W5527 Highway 106
P.O. Box 800
Fort Atkinson, Wisconsin 53538-0800
1-800-558-2110

© Leslie Cefali, 1999
Cover design: Frank Neu

The paper used in this publication meets the minimum requirements of American National Standard for Information Science — Permanence of Paper for Printed Library Material. ANSI/NISO Z39.48-1992.

Library of Congress Cataloging in Publication
    Cefali, Leslie.
      Cook-a-book : reading activities for grades Pre-K to 6 / Leslie Cefali.
    -- 2nd ed.
        p.   cm.
    Includes bibliographic references.
    ISBN 1-57950-001-3 (soft)
     1. Cookery. 2. Reading (Elementary). I. Title.
  TX652.C42
  641.5 ' 123 --dc21   99-22697
                                    CIP

Contents

Introduction to Second Edition

It's funny how old friends will unexpectedly appear in one's life. While walking through Printer's Row, an old and rare book fair in Chicago one summer afternoon, I ran into an old, almost forgotten companion. The book, *The Boy Who Ate Flowers* (see page 79 for recipe), was sitting on a table among other rare books at a booth at the end of the street. I immediately recognized this book, as it was one I had owned as a child. It was one of the first books, other than the ever present Golden Books, that I owned as my very own. That is me in the photograph, clutching the book that I had just received as a Christmas present many years ago. This book, unlike the Golden Books was like a library book, a *real* book, with a hard cover and big wonderful, colorful pages —and it *belonged* to me!

Little did I know when I had that book read and reread to me, that years later I would write a book about cooking and about books. This time I wouldn't be like the boy who ate flowers, but a lover of reading and a person who devoured books! Who knows, maybe *Cook-A-Book* got its early germination as I enjoyed *The Boy Who Ate Flowers* . Now once again a copy of this book has a special place of honor on my book shelves, right next to the photograph of the little girl, with her sister and grandfather… the little girl who would someday write *Cook-A-Book* and find a familiar friend among the old and rare books. Happy "R'eating!"

Notes to Readers

On Serving Sizes In creating these recipes with children, I have always thought that the literature, not the food was the most important part of the whole experience. Therefore, serving size of each recipe is designed to be a sample of the food eaten in the books, not a meal. Keeping this in mind, the recipes that do not include the number of servings will generally allow a class of 20 to 25 students to have a taste. Often times I have doubled the recipe if I wanted the children to have more.

On Reading Levels As an educator who firmly believes that a quality book can be shared and enjoyed with adults and children of all ages, I hesitantly have listed the books in *Cook-A-Book* by reading levels. Children of all ages can enjoy most of the books listed with an enthusiastic adult. Many of the chapter books work successfully with young children, and I have been equally successful using simpler picture books with intermediate students. The reading levels are very flexible and it is my hope that they will not stop you from sharing these books and recipes with children of all ages.

Reading levels are coded as: *ps*–preschool, *pm*–primary, *in*–intermediate, and *all ages.*

Introduction

The recipes in this book can be used at home or in the classroom to help children become involved with quality literature and reading. The books become a part of a child's life as the child makes the foods that are actually eaten in the book. When one boy in my class reminded me that we had to throw three kisses at the pasta pot before we took it off the heat, when we made pasta from scratch to extend the book *Strega Nona* by Tomie dePaola, I became aware that these activities helped the children "live" the story.

The importance of reading aloud to children is emphasized continually in educational research. The current study, Becoming a Nation of Readers: The Report of the Commission on Reading, by the National Academy of Education, The National Institute of Education, and The Center for the Study of Reading, states that the single most important activity for successful reading is reading aloud to children. Other current sources include the popular Read-Aloud Handbook by Jim Trelease, and the national television special entitled "Drop Everything and Read."

Cooking can be a great motivator in reading because the participants are totally immersed in language development, concept building, sequence skills, comprehension, and listening skills, resulting in a deeper involvement with books and literature. In addition to sharing quality literature through these recipes, cooking is important in a classroom because it covers the entire curriculum. Besides the language arts, it encompasses math, science, health, nutrition, and social studies. Cooking actively involves every child in a class or home regardless of his or her academic level.

Having cooking experiences that are centered around children's literature help make the books become "real" for children. Children need concrete learning experiences to get involved in the learning process. What better way for them to become a part of a book than to experience cooking and preparing food that is eaten in nursery rhymes and literature?

I have found that the books we use for cooking experiences are long remembered and cherished, even years later. These books are ones that the children will probably never forget.

> Books should not be viewed as ends in themselves but as windows that open through to new ideas and lead to more investigation, study, and recreation. When your children become more than superficially interested in books they read, their reading interests broaden and they are more likely to maintain their reading habit than if they merely jump from one book to another (*Growing Up Reading*, Linda Leonard Lamme, Acropolis Books, 1985, p. 163).

Besides offering the children fun, concrete, and meaningful relationships with books, cooking with books also benefits the parents and other family members. I always send home a note listing the books and activities that we have done in class. Many children will later tell me that they have reread the book and have often prepared the food at home with their parents. Several parents at conferences have made comments about the book-related cooking experiences, and some have even called years later to ask about a book or activity that we had done when their child was in my class.

All foods included in this book are taken directly from quality literature. Many of the books have received awards for their contributions to children's literature. My students have made jam with Sal and her mother in *Blueberries for Sal* and have eaten Turkish Delight with Eustace in *The Lion, the Witch and the Wardrobe*.

Though we cook often in my classroom during first semester, I try to "cook-a-book" regularly every week during the second semester. We spend a lot of time during the first part of the year reading many books, both those that we will use in cooking and many that we will not. When we do "cook-a-book," I want my children to be familiar with the story already. I want the cooking activity to further their enjoyment of the book, not to be the sole reason for it. My main purpose in these cooking experiences is to promote the enjoyment of books and reading. By second semester, I also know which parents are able and willing to help with the cooking experiences and the children are settled into a routine without too many holiday interruptions.

Some of the recipes in this book take more time than others. On days when I am feeling rushed, or I do not want to bring in a lot of ingredients, I will use (for example) the recipe listed with *Bread and Jam for Frances* by Russell Hoban. The children simply spread grape jam on pieces of bread. For this activity I simply have a mother, father, or other helper call the children over to a table two or three at a time during the morning when I am working with small groups and individual students. The cooking experience does not need to take up any more time in your day. This arrangement works equally well when the children are cooking with an oven or electric skillet.

I generally have a class size of 28 to 30 students. The secret in cooking with students is to be sure everyone has a chance to do something. My students will wait patiently if they know that they will have an important role in the activity. Be sure to have the students, not the adults, do most of the work—stirring, cracking eggs, pouring, kneading, cutting. It is extremely important that the children help with even the smallest contribution. If you have 30 students, stir your batter 30 times.

When I first began teaching and cooking in my classroom, I would bring my ingredients and all my kitchen supplies the day we were cooking. Almost every time I would leave something important at home, such as the colander, a potholder, or even the pot! I now have a small cabinet at school to store all my supplies. Some of the kitchen utensils were extras I had at home; others were picked up at garage sales or secondhand stores, and still others were donated by parents. A note sent home explaining what you need donated is usually effective.

Supply List

Here is a list of cooking supplies that I keep at school:

- plastic silverware (about 30 knives, forks and spoons)
- electric skillet
- 2 rectangular cake pans
- 2 square cake pans
- 1 cookie sheet
- 1 saucepan with lid
- 1 hot plate (an electrical appliance similar to a stove burner)
- 1 colander
- 4 metal mixing bowls, various sizes
- 1 popcorn popper (the older model that you can cook in)
- 1 potato masher
- 1 timer
- 3 or 4 sets of measuring spoons
- 2 or 3 sets of measuring cups, both dry and liquid
- 1 ladle
- 1 spatula
- several metal forks, knives and spoons
- 2 large cutting boards
- 3 wooden spoons
- 10 sharp knives
- 1 bottle opener
- 1 can opener
- 2 or 3 sets of dish cloths and towels
- 2 or 3 hot mats
- 35 plastic coffee cups
- several packages of paper cups
- napkins
- food coloring
- foil cupcake liners
- paper plates
- 1 small electric oven (We usually use the oven in the school kitchen when we have a lot to bake.)
- dish soap

Happy cooking—and most importantly, happy reading!

Acknowledgments

Thank you to all the children who have helped me cook so many of these recipes through the years. Thank you to the children, parents and teachers at Flint Lake Elementary School in Valparaiso, Indiana, who allowed me to work with them to get such wonderful illustrations for this edition. Thank you to my husband, Jeff, a talented cook, who encourages me, helps edit my manuscripts, and does the real cooking in our home, so I have time to write, create and dream. And thanks to my mom, Joan Farr Nordstrom, for all the support and for introducing my to The Boy Who Ate the Flowers.

Illustrations provided by the following students:

Recipe Divider
Julie Alexander

Eggs
Evan Costas
Beth Maack
Jennifer Dinkelman
Kim Abcouwer
Andrea Stout

Cereal, Oatmeal
Andreas Shepard
Robbie Martin
Shane Sewell
Ashley Tyman
Katie Horan
Lindsey Waelde

Pancakes, Latkes
Will Howell
Laura Nietert
John VanVlict
Takashi Irieda
Jackie Evan

Breads, Rolls, Muffins
Joey Zic
Jamie Clarke
Lindsey Nelson
Kelsey Marchak
Kyle Annen
Kara Strehler
Deanne Smrzlick
Michael Westfall
Ross Bunchek
Evan Yuriga
Melissa Webb
Robert Perry
Nick Kopack
Brian Goodaker
Danielle Waugh
Alex Petersen
Ben Hamilton
Tim Harreld
Jessica Mueller
Joshua Bridgewater
John Cribbs

Spreads, Sauces
Evan Christian
Lauren Crandall
Julie Alexander
Andrew Leeth
Jeff Jensen
Kevin Piet

Sandwiches, Tacos
Michele Loudermilk
Matt Bradney
Jackie Evan
Dani Heuring
Nicholas Puaca
Katie Letcher

Chili, Soups, Stews
Meagan Arizpe
Leah Bess
Georgia Kouknas
David Stück
Sarah Goodaker
Dever Thomas
Amanda Thomas
Heather Delecki
Zachary Rocha
Joe Cempel
Ashley Henderson
Andrew Bilheimer

Pizza
Carl Rivera
Ryan Miller
Melissa Lyon

Pasta, Rice
Sam Brown
Christina Taylor
Alu Olar
Dustin Gahimer
Daniel Petkovic
Katie Hood

Fish, Meat
Allie Zikesch
Christian Demko
Zach Schuta

Laura Wunder
Alex Fusak
Jessica Strainis
Kyle Annen
Kyle Jacques
Brandon Tritle

Fruits, Vegetables
Matt Davis
Kaitlin Kearby
Adam Robinson
Alexandra
Andrejevich
Jim Wring
Kyle Klein
Jordan Bridgewater
Billy Hedrick
Tiffany Sandberg
Paul Jaskowiak
Kirsten Anderson
Zach Rodenbarger
Matt Lewis
Colleen Ennes
Jarrod Carr
Rebekah Niedner
Nicole Collins
Katie Kleemann
Chelsey Dunleavy

Cookies, Candy
Stephen Bilheimer
Kara Lonadier
Rachel Holmgren
Samantha Haller
Trenton Redington
Ben Shuta
Beth Maack
Hannah Coatsolonia

Cakes, Tarts
Vinnie Santolino
Briana Ouderkirk
Candace Pederson
Amy Stipp
Ed Wake
Natalie Novello

Anna Kispert
Whitney Wojtkowski
Jakob Zetterberg
Hanna Mueller
Jill Bennett

Pies
Ashley Budd
Ross Ryan
Kevin Morse
Fay Gammon
Aaron Cavanaugh
Zac Cunningham
Leeann St. John

Ice Cream
Patrick Bushbaum
Laura Grayam

Beverages
Natalie Moldstad
Ashley Hoffman
Alyssa Finley
Brian Schwager
Janelle Elwood
Jennie Evan
Marissa Kimsey
Hayley Gerstler

Celebrations
Michael Tilleman
Nicole Nuzzo
Trenton Redington
Emily Baas
Nicole Persley
Anna Bianco
Sydney Coatsolonia
Kyle Sims
Eric Martin
Katie Lenz
Travis Allen
Tanav Popli
Kevin Ribordy
Matt Vilga
Joe Corsbie

 Eggs

This Is the Way We Eat Our Lunch
Edith Bauer • Illustrated by Steve Bjorkman
Scholastic, 1995

Children from around the world are introduced along with the foods they like to eat. Chowder from Massachusetts; hot dogs from New York; fried plantain, grown and eaten in Puerto Rico; and Bubble and Squeak from England are all mentioned. Twenty-two places around the world are mentioned in rhymed couplets. The book includes recipes for three of the foods mentioned: fruit salad, hummus and wild rice soup. Try these or the one below. *(ps, pm)*

Souffle

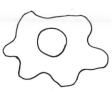

- ½ cup grated cheddar cheese
- 2 tablespoons olive oil
- 1 cup milk
- 3 eggs, separated
- salt and pepper to taste

Heat the oil and mix in flour until well blended. Stir in milk. Bring to a boil. Add grated cheese. Heat on low until cheese melts. Separate eggs. Add the 3 egg yolks to the cheese mixture and heat on low until yolks start to firm up. Let cool. In a separate bowl, combine egg whites with salt and pepper. Beat until stiff. Add egg whites to the yolk and cheese mixture. Fold into ungreased casserole dish. Bake at 325° for 25 to 30 minutes until firm.

More recipes for this book on pages 28, 42, 59, 73, 103.

The Seven Silly Eaters
Mary Ann Hoberman • Illustrated by Marla Frazee
Harcourt Brace, 1997

Mrs. Peters has seven silly eaters. Each of her seven children has a particular food that they will eat, *and* each has to be prepared a special way. Peter will only drink milk at a certain temperature, Lucy will only drink pink lemonade—homemade! Jack prefers applesauce and the twins want only eggs—one poached, the other fried. When Mrs. Peters' birthday comes along the children make her a special cake, each adding their food of choice. *(ps, pm)*

Fried Egg

Have each child crack an egg in a skillet—try not to break the yolk! Fry in a teaspoon of vegetable oil until it starts to turn a golden brown on the bottom and along the edges. Flip the egg and continue to cook on low until the second side begins to brown.

Poached Egg

Put 3 to 4 cups of water in a skillet. Bring to a boil and turn down heat. Crack egg into water trying not to break the yolk. Cover and cook 3 to 4 minutes. Salt and pepper to taste.

More recipes for this book on pages 6, 69, 110.

Green Eggs and Ham

Dr. Seuss
Random House, 1960

Do you like green eggs and ham?

Green Eggs and Ham

- 1 egg per child
- green food coloring
- 1 pkg. sliced ham
- 1 tablespoon butter or margarine

Have each child crack an egg into a small bowl. Add a drop or two of green food coloring and scramble it up well. Add this egg to a larger bowl that will hold all eggs to be cooked. Cut the sliced ham into half-inch squares. Melt the butter in an electric skillet. Add eggs and cook. When eggs are just about set, add the diced ham pieces. *(ps, pm)*

"Would you eat them in a car?"

Gregory the Terrible Eater

Mitchell Sharmat • Illustrated by Jose Aruego and Ariane Dewey
Scholastic, 1980 ✶ Reading Rainbow Selection

Gregory is a goat and his parents are concerned about his eating habits. They think he should eat good foods like tin cans and the evening newspaper, instead of junk food like fruits, vegetables, and eggs. Finally they compromise. Gregory agrees to eat scrambled eggs, orange juice, and a piece of waxed paper. Even though Gregory's parents won't let him skip the waxed paper, you might wish to allow your students to do so! *(ps, pm)*

Scrambled Eggs

Let each child crack an egg and scramble it in a small bowl. Many children have never had the opportunity to crack their own egg and this is an important part of cooking this recipe. After scrambling their individual eggs, let children pour them in a large bowl. For each dozen, add ¼ to ½ cup of milk to the egg mixture. Melt 2 tablespoons of butter in an electric skillet and scramble eggs until they are set. Serve each child an egg and a glass of orange juice.

More recipes for this book on page 110.

Scrambled Eggs Super!

Dr. Seuss
Random House, 1953

Peter T. Hooper gathers hundreds of eggs from hundreds of very unusual birds to make Scrambled eggs Super–dee–Dooper–dee–Booper, Special de luxe–a–la Peter T. Hooper. To make your scrambled eggs Super–dee–Dooper, add onions, green peppers, cheese and ham. *(ps, pm)*

Special Deluxe Scrambled Eggs

- 1 egg per child
- ⅓ cup milk
- 1 tablespoon butter
- 4 ozs. cheddar cheese, grated

- 1 onion, diced
- 1 green pepper, diced
- 1 pkg. ham, cubed

Let children grate cheese and cut up ham and vegetables. Have each child crack and mix his or her own egg and put it into a large mixing bowl. Add milk. Melt butter in skillet. Saute onions and green peppers until tender. Add eggs and cook until set, adding cheese at the last minute.

The Man Who Tried to Save Time

Phyllis Krasilovsky • Illustrated by Marcia Sewell
Doubleday, 1979

Once there was a man who lived in a little house with his cat. He cleans his house, tends his garden, and goes to the office on a regular schedule every day. One day he decides to to do all these things faster, so he can have time to just sit in his chair and rock. He eats his breakfast before going to bed and goes to sleep with his clothes on so he can save time in the morning. After a while he realizes that he likes his old way best. He returns to his regular schedule, which, among other things, includes eating his breakfast of orange juice, toast, and eggs in the morning. *(ps, pm)*

Orange Juice, Toast, and Eggs

Divide your class into three groups. The first group makes frozen orange juice, or squeezes oranges for fresh juice. The second group makes and butters a piece of toast for each child. The third group cracks, cooks, and serves one scrambled egg per student.

Banbury Fair

Traditional Mother Goose

As I was going to Banbury,
Upon a summer's day,
My dame had butter, eggs, and fruit,
And I had corn and hay.

Eggs

You will need 1 egg per child. Put the eggs in a large pot and cover them completely with water. Boil 12 to 15 minutes.

More recipes for this book on page 74.

Down Buttermilk Lane

Barbara Mitchell • Illustrated by John Sandford
See main entry on page 100

Red Beet Eggs

- 12 eggs
- 1 can sliced beets
- ½ cup vinegar
- ⅓ cup sugar
- ⅛ teaspoon celery salt
- ⅛ teaspoon allspice

Hard boil the eggs. Remove the egg shells. Add remaining ingredients to a pan. Add ½ cup of beet juice from can. If there is not enough juice to make ½ cup, add water. Heat to a boil. Put mixture in a bowl. Add eggs and allow to cool. Refrigerate 24 hours before serving. Turn the eggs several times while they marinate to make sure they all dye evenly.

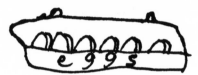

Cereal, Oatmeal

The Magic Porridge Pot
Traditional Folktale

A little girl and her widowed mother are given a magic pot. The pot starts and stops cooking porridge on command, with the proper magic words. One day when the little girl is gone, her mother prepares some porridge. The mother forgets the magic words to turn off the pot. Before long, porridge flows from her house and out onto the streets of the town. Will the magic pot ever stop making porridge? You might want to read this story and have your students compare it with Tomie dePaola's *Strega Nona*. *(all ages)*

Porridge

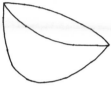

For each child you will need:

- 1 cup water
- ⅛ teaspoon salt
- ⅓ cup oat bran cereal

Mix the ingredients. Heat to a boil, stirring constantly. Reduce to low heat and cook for 1 to 2 minutes. Serve with brown sugar, cinnamon, raisins, or apple pieces if desired.

Pease Porridge Hot
Traditional Mother Goose

Pease porridge hot.
Pease porridge cold.
Pease porridge in a pot
Nine days old.

Some like it hot,
Some like it cold.
Some like it in a pot
Nine days old.

Porridge

For each child you will need:

- ¾ cup water
- ⅛ teaspoon salt
- 2½ tablespoons instant hot cereal

Heat water and salt until water just starts to boil. Stir in cereal. Cook 30 seconds. Remove from heat and let stand about a minute. For a creamier consistency, use milk instead of water.

Goldilocks and the Three Bears

Retold and illustrated by Jan Brett
Dodd, Mead, 1987

Jan Brett does a beautiful rendition of this classic fairy tale. This version is not to be missed! *(all ages)*

Porridge

For each child you will need:

- ¾ cup water
- ⅛ teaspoon salt
- ⅓ cup old-fashioned rolled oats
- raisins
- brown sugar
- milk

Bring the water to a boil. Add salt and oats. Cook for 5 minutes, stirring occasionally. Let stand a few minutes to thicken before serving. Add raisins, brown sugar, and milk if desired.

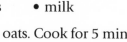

The Seven Silly Eaters

Mary Ann Hoberman • Illustrated by Marla Frazee
See main entry on page 1

Oatmeal

Prepare oatmeal by following the recipe on the oatmeal box or see below for a recipe.

Journey to America

Sonia Levitin
Atheneum, 1970

The Nazis are moving into Germany and Lisa Platt's father must leave for America. Lisa, her mother, and two sisters must wait in Switzerland for their father to send for them. The hardships of the war are shared in this work of historical fiction. The only food many have to eat is oatmeal—for breakfast, lunch, and dinner. One evening, all Lisa has to eat are oatmeal, crackers, and a half an apple. Another meal consists of oatmeal and beans. Cook these meals in class to allow your children to imagine what meals were like during this war. *(pm, in)*

Oatmeal

For each child you will need:

- ¾ cup water
- ⅛ teaspoon salt
- ⅓ cup old-fashioned rolled oats

Bring water to a boil. Add salt and oatmeal. Cook for 5 minutes, stirring constantly. Let stand a few minutes to thicken before serving. Serve with half an apple.

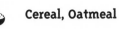

Pablo Remembers
George Ancona
Lothrop, Lee & Shepard, 1993

Beautifully illustrated with bright photographs, *Pablo Remembers* explains the three-day Mexican holiday—Fiesta del Día de los Muertos—or, The Day of the Dead. The holiday takes on more meaning for the reader as Pablo explains why this year's festival is important to him and his family. A recipe for atole follows. Recipes for a number of other foods mentioned, such as pan de muertos, hot chocolate, chicken, and tortillas are elsewhere in *Cook-A-Book*. *(pm, in)*

Atole

- 2 cups water
- 1/2 teaspoon cinnamon
- pinch of salt
- 1 cup cornmeal (yellow, white, or blue)
- 3 cups milk
- ½ cup honey

Mix cornmeal, water, salt and cinnamon in a pan. Stirring constantly, bring to a boil. When the liquid boils turn to low heat. Add milk and honey, stirring as you do. Continue to stir until it stops boiling. Do not reboil.

More recipes for this book on page 24.

If I Could Be My Grandmother
Steven Kroll, Illustrated by Lady McCrady
Pantheon, 1977

What would you do if you were a grandmother? The little girl in this book role plays all the things she would do. She would bake cookies and have cornflakes for breakfast. Find out what your students would do if they were grandparents. *(ps, pm)*

Cornflakes

Serve cornflakes with milk and sugar. Each child can prepare his or her own bowl of cereal.

More recipes for this book on page 86.

The Cereal Box
David McPhail
Little, Brown, 1974

Breakfast in this household is a real adventure. Everyone eats a different kind of cereal. The cereal the little boy eats is in a green box and it seems to contain more than just cereal! There's a pair of glasses, a live frog, a bird, and other surprises. There's even a creature with one eye! *(ps, pm)*

Cereal

Bring in dry cereal packaged in a green box or ask your students to. See how many different kinds of cereal you get. Serve with milk and sugar, and let children select the kind of cereal they want. Be sure to check the boxes for one-eyed monsters!

Pancakes, Latkes

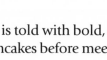

Sunday

Synthia Saint James
Albert Whitman, 1996

Sunday is for families and this family story of spending Sundays together is told with bold, colorful illustrations and simple text. After sleeping late the family enjoys pancakes before meeting Grandma and Grandpa at church. *(ps, pm)*

Pancakes

- ⅔ cup flour
- 2 teaspoons baking powder
- ¼ teaspoon salt
- 1 teaspoon vanilla
- 1 egg
- ½ cup milk or buttermilk
- 1 tablespoon vegetable oil

Sift together flour, baking powder, salt and sugar. In a separate bowl, beat the egg. Mix milk and oil with egg. Add egg mixture to the flour mixture. Stir until dry ingredients are moistened. Pour batter into a greased skillet, turning each pancake once.

Grandma Essie's Covered Wagon

David Williams • Illustrated by Wiktor Sadowski
Knopf, 1993

For as long as he could remember, author David Williams' grandmother, Essie, had been sharing the memories of her childhood travels in a covered wagon with him. In 1988, when Essie was 87 years old, David told her he would like to capture those memories in a book. The details she shared became *Grandma Essie's Covered Wagon*, a story told mostly in Essie's own words. *(pm, in)*

Pancakes

- 1 teaspoon baking soda
- 2½ cups buttermilk
- 1 cup white flour
- 1 cup barley flour
- 1 cup cornmeal
- 1 tablespoon butter
- 1 tablespoon sugar
- 2 eggs, beaten
- ½ teaspoon salt

Mix baking soda and buttermilk. In a separate bowl mix white flour, barley flour, and cornmeal together. Cream butter and sugar. Add salt, eggs and buttermilk mixture to butter and sugar. Slowly add dry ingredients. Pour batter in a bit of hot oil in a skillet. Turn when pancake starts to bubble and get puffy. Cook remaining side until golden brown.

Note: If you choose not to use this recipe, make sure to find another that makes pancakes from scratch, not a mix. The book makes a point to say that the pancakes were made from scratch.

The Sugaring Off Party
Jonathon London • Illustrated by Giles Pelletier
Dutton Children's Books, 1995

On the night before her 60th sugaring off party, Grand-mere reminisces about her first party. She talks with her grandson, Paul, who is about to experience his first party. It is March and the sap in the maple trees is starting to run. This means it is time for family and friends to gather to make maple syrup. French words are interspersed throughout this story which takes place in Canada.

If you are fortunate enough to live in the North check for maple sugar events during February and March. Look for parks or historical sites where they gather the sap and boil it down to make syrup that you can enjoy with pancakes. *(pm, in)*

Pancakes   Use one of the recipes in this section and serve with *real* maple syrup.

More recipes for this book on page 80.

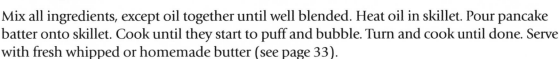

The Story of the Little Babaji
Helen Bannerman • Illustrated by Fred Marcellino
HarperCollins, 1996

This story was originally written by Helen Bannerman in 1899 and entitled *Little Black Sambo*. In this revision, the characters have been given authentic Indian names to more closely represent the story's setting in India. As in the original story, tigers are tricked by the main character into running around the base of a tree. The result is that the tigers are churned into butter, and Babaji's mother uses the tiger butter with pancakes. *(all ages)*

Pancakes

- 1 egg, beaten
- 1 cup self rising flour
- ¾ cup milk
- 1 teaspoon vanilla
- 2 tablespoons vegetable oil

Mix all ingredients, except oil together until well blended. Heat oil in skillet. Pour pancake batter onto skillet. Cook until they start to puff and bubble. Turn and cook until done. Serve with fresh whipped or homemade butter (see page 33).

Pancakes, Pancakes
Eric Carle
Knopf, 1970

Jack wants pancakes for breakfast and helps his mother make them. He goes to the mill for the flour, to the henhouse for eggs, to the meadow to milk the cow. He makes butter, gathers wood for the fire, and goes to the cellar for the homemade jam. This story, like *Pancakes for Breakfast* by Tomie dePaola, shows where many of our breakfast foods come from. Make as much as you can from scratch. Recipes for all the foods are listed elsewhere in *Cook-A-Book*. The recipe on the next page is for pancakes. Eat them with strawberry jam, as Jack does in the book. *(all ages)*

Pancakes

- ¼ stick butter
- 2 cups milk
- pinch of salt
- 2 eggs
- ⅓ cup sugar
- 1 cup flour

Melt butter and mix with milk, salt, eggs, and sugar. Add flour and blend well. Cook pancakes in a very hot skillet. Serve with butter and strawberry jam.

If You Give a Pig a Pancake

Laura Joffe Numeroff • Illustrated by Felcia Bond
Scholastic, 1998

Following the predictable pattern made popular by her previous books, *If You Give a Mouse a Cookie* and *If You Give a Moose a Muffin,* Numeroff presents another book, this time about a pig and a pancake. What would happen if you gave a pig one of the pancakes you and children make? *(ps, pm)*

Pancakes   Follow one of the many recipes for pancakes found in this section.

Brown Cow, Green Grass, Yellow Mellow Sun

Ellen Jackson • Illustrated by Victoria Raymond
Hyperion, 1995

Simple text explains how the yellow sun warms the earth, how a brown cow eats green grass and gives milk, and how a child and his granny churn the milk into butter. *(ps, pm)*

Big Brown Pancakes

Author Ellen Jackson provides recipes for Big Brown Pancakes and Yellow Mellow Butter at the end of the story. You may want to use these recipes or try one of the pancake recipes in this section with the homemade butter found on page 33.

The Blueberry Bears

Eleanor Lapp • Illustrated by Margot Apple
Albert Whitman, 1983

Bessie Allen picked and picked the blueberries that grew behind her cabin. She froze them, canned them, made pies, muffins, and pancakes with them. You can enjoy the blueberry muffin recipe in the book or make some blueberry pancakes. Just be sure to leave some in the patch for the bears! *(ps, pm)*

Blueberry Pancakes

- 1 egg, beaten
- 1 cup milk
- 2 tablespoons oil
- 1¼ cups flour
- 1 tablespoon sugar
- 3 teaspoons baking powder
- ½ teaspoon salt
- blueberries

Combine egg, milk, and oil. Add dry ingredients; mix well. Pour batter into hot, greased skillet. When pancakes bubble, add blueberries to each pancake, turn and cook the other side until golden brown. Serve with butter and syrup.

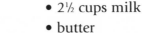

Johnny-Cake

Joseph Jacobs
G. P. Putnam, 1933

Johnny-Cake, like the gingerbread boy, pops out of the oven while he is being cooked. This is another one of many variations on this theme. When you make a johnny-cake, try to eat him before he escapes down the hallway! *(all ages)*

Johnny-Cake

- 4 cups biscuit mix
- 2 eggs
- 2½ cups milk
- butter

Mix the biscuit mix and eggs. Gradually add milk and mix until smooth. Add more milk if the batter needs to be a bit thinner. Melt butter in skillet. Pour batter making 2 to 3 inch pancakes. Turn pancakes when bubbles appear. Cook other side until brown. Serve warm with butter and syrup or jam.

The Pancake

Anita Lobel
Greenwillow, 1978

Here is yet another book based on the theme of runaway food. This time a pancake runs away from a woman, her seven children, her husband, and several farm animals. It is a pig in this book who finally catches the pancake and eats him. The woman takes the whole gang, including the animals, back home and makes another pancake, and they all eat him before he gets away. *(all ages)*

Pancakes

- 2 cups flour
- 4 teaspoons baking powder
- 2 tablespoons sugar
- 1 teaspoon salt
- 1½ cups milk
- 2 eggs, beaten
- 4 tablespoons melted butter

Sift the dry ingredients into a bowl. Blend milk, eggs, and butter in a separate bowl, then mix with the dry ingredients. Drop batter by the spoonful onto a hot skillet. Turn when bubbles appear on the pancakes. Cook other side until golden brown.

Journey Cake, Ho

Ruth Sawyer • Illustrated by Robert McCloskey
Viking, 1953 ★ Caldecott Honor Book

This book is another version of the gingerbread man story. This time it is a journey cake or pancake that tries to escape from a parade of characters who want to eat him for dinner. *(all ages)*

Journey Cake

- 1½ cups cornmeal
- 1 teaspoon baking powder
- ½ teaspoon salt
- 3 eggs
- 1 cup milk
- ½ cup shortening
- 1 tablespoon sugar
- 1½ cups flour

Sift together cornmeal, baking powder, and salt. Add eggs, beating well after each one. Add milk, shortening, and dry ingredients. Spoon batter onto hot, greased skillet. Turn cakes when they start to bubble. Cook other side until brown. Serve with syrup—if they don't run away!

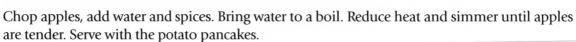

Mrs. Katz and Tush

Patricia Polacco
See main entry on page 63

Spicy Chopped Apples with Potato Pancakes

Using one of the latke recipes in this section, have the class make potato pancakes. Serve them with hot spiced apples.

- 5–6 apples
- 1 teaspoon cinnamon
- 1 teaspoon allspice
- water to cover

Chop apples, add water and spices. Bring water to a boil. Reduce heat and simmer until apples are tender. Serve with the potato pancakes.

Tuck Everlasting

Natalie Babbitt
Farrar, Straus, & Giroux, 1975

Winnie Foster discovers a fascinating secret about Miles Tuck and his family who never seem to age. This book will spark an engaging discussion about the advantages and disadvantages of living forever. Winnie eats supper with the Tuck's when they have flapjacks, bacon, bread, and applesauce. *(in)*

Flapjacks

- 3 eggs
- 2½ cups buttermilk
- 1 teaspoon baking powder
- 1 teaspoon baking soda
- ½ teaspoon salt
- 2–2½ cups flour
- 2 tablespoons oil

Beat eggs; add milk. Mix dry ingredients in separate bowl. Slowly add dry ingredients to milk-and-egg mixture. Add oil and mix well. Pour batter onto a hot greased skillet. When bubbles appear on pancakes, turn and cook until second side is golden brown. Serve warm with syrup. To duplicate the Tucks' meal, also fry a piece of bacon for each child. Serve bread and applesauce to complete the meal.

Harvest Song

Ron Hirschi • Illustrated by Deborah Haeffele
Cobblehill Dutton, 1991

Set in a gentler time, a young girl describes planting a potato garden on her grandmother's farm. When the potato plants begin to grow, she and grandmother have a picnic of yellow cheese, crunchy apples and fresh baked bread. Later when fall arrives, the potatoes are ready to harvest. *(all ages)*

"One potato for the springtime;
Two for summer sun.
Golden potatoes for wintertime,
Now our work is done. "

Potato Cakes   See recipes in this section for potato pancakes or latkes.

More recipes for this book on page 18.

Laughing Latkes

M. B. Goffstein
Farrar, Straus, & Giroux, 1980

Do latkes laugh when you eat them with sour cream? Latkes are a traditional Hanukkah meal. These potato pancakes are good to eat while celebrating the holidays in December, or anytime during the year. *(ps, pm)*

Latkes

- 5 large potatoes
- 1 small onion
- ½ teaspoon baking powder
- 1 teaspoon salt
- 2 eggs
- 1½ tablespoons flour

Scrub the potatoes. Using a cheese grater, let the children grate the potatoes and onion. Mix in baking powder, salt, eggs, and flour. Using a tablespoon, pour batter into a hot greased electric skillet. Serve with sour cream or applesauce. Makes about 45 to 50 small latkes.

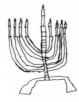

Grandma's Latkes

Malka Drucker • Illustrated by Eve Chwast
Harcourt Brace Jovanovich, 1992

Another Hanukkah book to share during December, here Grandma shares stories and latkes. You can make the recipe included at the end of *Grandma's Latkes*, or you may make the ones here. *(all ages)*

Latkes

- 6 medium potatoes, peeled
- 1 onion
- 2 eggs
- 2 tablespoons flour
- 1 teaspoon salt
- ¼ teaspoon baking powder
- vegetable oil

Grate potatoes and onions. This could be done quickly in a food processor, or the children can grate them by hand with a cheese grater. Stir in remaining ingredients, except the oil. Drop mixture, by spoonfuls, into hot oil in a skillet. Fry until golden brown, flip and fry again. Drain in paper towels. Serve warm with applesauce or sour cream.

Inside-Out Grandma

Joan Rothenberg
Hyperion, 1995

When Grandma has her clothes on inside out, Rosie discovers it's to remind her grandmother to buy oil for latkes. Wearing her clothes inside out reminds Grandma of Rosie's dad when he was little. Rosie's dad reminds Grandma of Grandpa Rueben, which reminds her of copper red hair, and on and on. As Grandma explains the meanings of all her reminders, she shares family stories and Hanukkah memories with Rosie. *(all ages)*

There is a recipe for latkes in *Inside-Out Grandma*, or you may want to try one of the latke recipes here.

Latkes

- 6 potatoes
- 1 onion
- 2 eggs, beaten
- ½ cup matzo meal
- 1 teaspoon salt
- vegetable oil

Grate potatoes and onion in a food processor, or have the children grate the potatoes by hand with a cheese grater. Drain water from potatoes, squeezing out as much liquid as possible. Add eggs, matzo meal and salt. Heat about 1 inch of vegetable oil in a skillet. Drop potato mixture by the spoonful into the oil and cook until golden brown, turning once. It should take a minute or two on each side. Add oil to skillet as needed. Serve latkes hot with applesauce or sour cream.

The Miracle of the Potato Latkes
Malka Penn • Illustrated by Giora Carmi
Holiday House, 1994

Tante Golda is well known for making the best latkes in all of Russia. She shares the potato pancakes with her friends and neighbors all year. One year a severe drought leaves Tante and her friends without potatoes to make latkes. Tante believes "God will provide," which he does as potatoes are mysteriously left for her—a true miracle. *(all ages)*

A recipe for latkes is included at the end of the story. You can make that recipe or try this one.

Latkes

- 3 large potatoes
- 1 onion
- 2 eggs
- ½ cup flour
- ¾ teaspoon salt
- pepper, to taste
- vegetable oil

Grate potatoes and onion by hand with a cheese grater, or quickly in a food processor. Add eggs and mix well. Stir in dry ingredients. Heat oil in a frying pan and fry small latkes until golden brown on each side.

You can also make latkes after reading:
All the Lights in the Night by Arthur A. Levine. Tambourine Books, 1991.
Just Enough Is Plenty by Barbara Diamond Goldin. Viking Kestrel, 1988.
Hanukkah by Roni Schotter. Little, Brown, 1990.

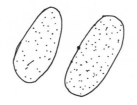

Breads, Rolls, Muffins

Make Me a Peanut Butter Sandwich and a Glass of Milk
Ken Robbins
Scholastic, 1992

Author Ken Robbins uses color-tinted photos to illustrate this nonfiction book that shows how grain is grown for bread, how peanuts are raised for peanut butter and how cows are milked. The "recipe" you use with this book can be as simple as making a peanut butter sandwich and serving it with a glass of milk, or as complex as visiting a dairy farm and bringing home fresh milk; making homemade bread; and grinding fresh peanut butter. If you choose to make everything from scratch, see the recipe on page 34 for making peanut butter. And enjoy the aroma from this bread as it bakes in your oven. *(all ages)*

Homemade Bread

- 2 cups boiling water
- ½ cup sugar
- ½ cup butter
- 1 pkg. dry yeast
- 1 teaspoon sugar
- ½ cup warm water
- 4 eggs
- ¼ teaspoon salt
- 8–10 cups flour

In a mixing bowl, pour boiling water over sugar and butter. Let sit until lukewarm. Dissolve 1 teaspoon sugar and the yeast in ½ cup warm water. Add to sugar and butter mixture. Mix in eggs and salt. Add flour one cup at a time until a stiff dough forms. Cover and let rise in the refrigerator until it is doubled in size. This may take several hours. You can leave the dough in the refrigerator and make the loaves the next day.

When the dough has doubled in size, punch it down and divide into loaves. Put in well-greased bread pans. Let dough rise a second time to double its size, this time at room temperature—about 2 to 3 hours. Bake at 425° for 10 minutes, reduce heat to 350° and bake for 30 more minutes. Cool before taking out of pans.

The Giant Jam Sandwich
John Vernon Lord
Houghton Mifflin, 1972

When four million wasps fly into Itching Down, the residents do all they can to get rid of them. They finally decide to make a giant jam sandwich. They bake the bread and bring in strawberry jam by the truckload.

At some delicatessens you can order fresh bread as long as five feet or longer! If you can order such a loaf, your students would enjoy spreading strawberry jam on it. If you would like to bake your own bread—not quite so large—this is a batter bread that does not have to be kneaded. *(ps, pm)*

Bread

- 2¾–3½ cups flour
- 1½ teaspoons salt
- ½ cup wheat germ
- 2 pkgs. quick-rise yeast
- 2 tablespoons oil
- 1½ cups very hot water
- 2 tablespoons molasses

Mix 1 cup flour with salt, wheat germ, and yeast. Add oil. Gradually add water and molasses to flour mixture and beat 3 minutes at medium speed with an electric mixer. Add ½ cup flour. Beat at high speed. Add enough flour to make a stiff batter. Cover and let rise in a warm, draft-free place until dough doubles in size—about 30 minutes.

Punch down batter. Beat for about 30 seconds. Turn into a greased 1½ quart casserole dish. Let rise again about 30 minutes. Bake at 375° for 45 minutes. Remove from casserole dish and cool.

The Little Red Hen
Traditional Fairy Tale

The little red hen plants the wheat, harvests the wheat, takes it to the mill to be ground into flour, and then bakes the bread. When she asks her friends to help, none of them will—that is, until they want to help her eat the warm bread! Arrange a trip to a flour mill or bakery, if possible. Your class will willingly help bake this bread! *(all ages)*

Whole Wheat Bread

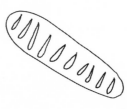

- 2 cups milk, scalded
- 2 tablespoons oil
- 2 tablespoons honey
- 1 tablespoon molasses
- 2 teaspoons salt
- 1 pkg. quick-rise yeast
- ¼ cup warm water
- about 5½ cups whole wheat flour

Combine milk, oil, honey, molasses, and salt. Mix well and cool to lukewarm. Dissolve yeast in water. Stir into mixture. Gradually add flour to make a stiff dough. Beat well each time you add more flour. Cover with damp towel. Put in a warm, draft-free area. Let dough rise until it is doubled. Punch down and knead on a floured surface until it is smooth and elastic. Divide dough in half and place in greased breadpans. Brush with melted butter. Cover and let rise until doubled in size again. Bake at 375° for 40 to 45 minutes. Remove from pans and cool.

Bread Is for Eating
David and Phillis Gershator • Illustrated by Emma Shaw-Smith
Henry Holt, 1995

El pan es para comer
El pan es para la vida
No tire el pan!
Ay, ay! Vida mía.

This Spanish song is interspersed with the story of bread—the planting of the seed, the harvesting of the wheat, the milling of the flour and the baking and eating of the bread. The music and translated English lyrics are included at the end of the book. The illustrations are done in the style of Guatemalan folk art and depict several types of bread. *(ps, pm)*

Bread

- 1 pkg. dry yeast
- 1¼ cups warm water
- 2 tablespoons honey
- 2 tablespoons oil
- 1 cup whole wheat flour
- 2 cups white flour

Grease bread pan with shortening or oil. Dissolve yeast in warm water. Add honey, shortening, whole wheat flour and ⅔ cup of white flour. Beat until smooth. Stir in the rest of the flour and beat until smooth. Cover and let rise about an hour. Stir down the dough. Place into greased bread pan. Let rise about 40 minutes until batter has doubled in size. Bake at 375° for 45 to 50 minutes, or until golden brown.

The Clever Hen
Traditional Mother Goose

I had a little hen, the prettiest ever seen;
She washed me the dishes and she kept the house clean.
She went to the mill to fetch me some flour;
She brought it home in less than an hour.
She baked me my bread, she brewed me my ale,
She sat by the fire and told many a fine tale.

Bread

If you want to bake bread from scratch, see the recipe listed with the book *The Little Red Hen* on page 17 or *The Giant Jam Sandwich* on pages 16-17. Another alternative is to buy frozen bread at the grocery store. Thaw the bread overnight in the refrigerator, or for 2 hours at room temperature. Place the thawed dough in greased loaf pans. Let rise in a draft-free area until the bread rises 1 inch over the top of the pans. Bake for 25 to 35 minutes at 350°.

Harvest Song
Ron Hirschi • Illustrated by Deborah Haeffele
See main entry on page 13

Fresh Baked Bread and Yellow Cheese and Apple Slices

Using a bread recipe found in this section, bake a loaf of bread with your class. Serve warm with a yellow cheese such as cheddar, American or cojack. Allow each child to cut an apple into slices and enjoy! If baking bread seems like more work than you can muster and yet you want to enjoy this book with food, buy a loaf of crusty bakery bread to share with the class.

The Sign of the Beaver

Elizabeth George Speare
Houghton Mifflin, 1983 ★ Newbery Honor Book

Left alone in his family's cabin in the Maine wilderness, 12-year-old Matt must learn to survive while he awaits his father's return. When he meets an Indian chief and his grandson, Attean, Matt learns a lot about wildness survival. Many months pass with no sign of Matt's family. Matt must decide whether to move on with Attean and his family, who have by now become like family to him, or to continue to wait for his own family, from whom he has not heard. *(in)*

Corn Cake

- 1¼ cups flour
- ¾ cup cornmeal
- 2 tablespoons sugar
- 4 teaspoons baking powder
- ½ teaspoon baking soda
- 1 teaspoon salt
- 1 cup milk
- 4 tablespoons oil
- 2 eggs

Mix dry ingredients. In a separate bowl, combine milk, oil, eggs; mix well. Add milk mixture to dry ingredients; stir well. Pour batter into greased 8-inch pan. Bake for 20 to 25 minutes at 425°. Serve with molasses to enjoy corn cake just as Matt did.

Dragonfly's Tale

Retold and illustrated by Kristina Rodanas
Clarion, 1991

This story is based on an ancient Zuni tale and is set in the village of Hawikuh in New Mexico. When the Corn Maiden sees the villagers wasting their food from a plentiful harvest she decides to teach them a lesson by bringing on a famine. A young boy and his sister save the village from starvation. *(pm, in)*

Corn Bread   A couple different recipes for corn bread can be found on page 20.

Grinding Corn into Meal

Bring in ears of dried corn. Make sure it's corn for human consumption, not field corn for farm animals or Indian corn. Have the children remove corn kernels from the ears. Using a stone metate, have the child grind the corn by hand into cornmeal. Use the cornmeal to make corn cakes or bread from one of the recipes here. Serve hot and drenched in honey like in the book.

Appalachia

Cynthia Rylant • Illustrated by Barry Moser
Harcourt Brace Jovanovich, 1991

Cynthia Rylant's text and Barry Moser's illustrations blend beautifully to describe the gentle, quiet lifestyle and customs of the people who live in Appalachia. *(pm, in)*

Corn Bread

- 2 eggs
- 1½ teaspoons sugar
- 1 cup cornmeal
- 1 cup milk
- 1 cup flour
- 2 tablespoons butter
- 3 teaspoons baking powder

Separate eggs. Beat yolks in a bowl; beat whites in a second bowl. Add sugar to egg yolks and mix well. Stir in milk, flour and cornmeal. Add remaining ingredients. Pour into well-greased pan. Bake at 425° until golden brown or about 20 to 25 minutes.

More recipes for this book on page 93.

The Pumpkin Man from Piney Creek

Darleen Bailey Beard • Illustrated by Laura Keller

See main entry on page 79

Corn Bread

- 1 cup milk
- 1 cup cornmeal
- 1 teaspoon salt
- ½ teaspoon sugar
- ½ cup flour
- 1 teaspoon baking powder
- 2 tablespoons butter, melted
- 3 eggs, separated

Scald milk; add cornmeal, stirring mixture until thickened. Remove from heat. Add remaining dry ingredients and melted butter. In a separate bowl, beat egg yolks. Add to pan. Mix well. Put in a greased casserole dish and bake at 350° for 30 minutes.

Cranberry Thanksgiving

Wende and Harry Devlin

Parents' Magazine Press, 1971

When Maggie and her grandmother have company for Thanksgiving dinner, grandmother's famous cranberry bread recipe disappears. Who could have taken it? Grandmother's famous recipe can be found in the book. Of course, it's such a guarded secret that you'll have to read the book to find it! Below is a recipe for a not-so-famous, but still delicious cranberry bread. *(pm, in)*

Cranberry Bread

- 2 cups flour
- ½ teaspoon salt
- 2 teaspoons baking powder
- ½ teaspoon baking soda
- 1 cup sugar
- ⅛ teaspoon cinnamon
- 1 egg, beaten
- 2 tablespoons oil
- 2 tablespoons hot water
- ¼ cup grated orange rind
- ½ cup orange juice
- 1 cup cranberries, cut up
- ½ cup chopped nuts

Mix flour, salt, baking powder, baking soda, sugar, and cinnamon. In a separate bowl, blend egg, oil, water, orange rind, and orange juice. Stir this mixture into dry ingredients. Add cranberries and nuts. Pour into two greased loaf pans. Bake for 1 hour and 10 minutes at 325°.

A Beekeeper's Year
Sylvia A. Johnson • Illustrated by Nick Von Ohlen
Little, Brown, 1994

A Beekeeper's Year is a nonfiction look at beekeeping. Colored photographs accompany text describing the beekeeper's protective clothing, tools and equipment. Recipes that use honey are provided. You can make honey/peanut butter spread, honey/chocolate coconut cookies, or cocoa with honey from the recipes in the book, or try this recipe for orange honey bread. *(pm, in)*

Orange Honey Bread

- ¼ cup butter
- ½ cup honey
- 1 egg
- 2 cups flour

- 2 teaspoons baking powder
- ¼ teaspoon baking soda
- ½ teaspoon salt
- 1 cup orange juice

Combine butter and honey in a bowl. Beat egg and add to the honey mixture. Add remaining ingredients. Mix well. Pour mixture into a greased 5x9-inch baking pan. Bake at 350° for 45 minutes to an hour or until inserted toothpick comes out clean. Cool and enjoy.

The Keeping Quilt
Patricia Polacco
Simon & Schuster, 1988

A quilt made with memories and fabrics from "the old country" is brought to America to comfort an immigrant Jewish family. The history of the quilt is shared as the family preserves its traditions at births, weddings, funerals and other family gatherings. At each event, the quilt plays an important role in the celebration. The story ends many, many years after the quilt's beginnings, with the birth of the author's daughter. *(all ages)*

Challah, a yeast bread enjoyed in the story, is often served with Sabbath meals. A recipe for chicken soup, also eaten by the author's family, appears on page 43.

Challah

- 1 package dry yeast
- 1 tablespoon sugar
- ⅓ cup water, lukewarm
- 1 teaspoon salt

- 5 tablespoons cooking oil
- 2 eggs, lightly beaten
- 5½ cups flour

Glaze

- poppy seeds
- 1 egg, beaten—add a pinch of salt and sugar

In a bowl, combine yeast and sugar. Stir in water. Add just enough flour to cover water. Cover bowl with a dish towel and set aside about 10 to 15 minutes, until mixture looks a bit foamy. Add salt, eggs and oil, mix well. Add enough flour to form a dough. Knead about 10 minutes, adding flour if dough is too sticky. (Dough should be soft, not firm.) Place dough in lightly greased bowl. Cover with dish towel and leave in a warm area. Let it rise until doubled in size, about an hour to an hour and a half. When doubled, knead dough again and return to bowl. Cover and let rise slowly in the refrigerator for 6 to 8 hours. Knead dough on a lightly floured surface again. Divide into 6 equal pieces. Roll each piece into a long rope about 18 inches long and 1 inch in diameter. Braid 3 pieces of dough together. Place on on a greased cookie sheet. Repeat with remaining dough. Cover loaves and let rise an hour, or until doubled in size. Brush with glaze and sprinkle with poppy seeds. Bake at 375° for 40 minutes or until brown.

Kulich *(A Russian Easter Bread)*

- 2 packages dry yeast
- ½ cup warm water
- ¾ cup lukewarm milk
- ⅓ cup sugar
- ½ teaspoon salt
- 2 eggs
- ½ cup shortening
- ½ cup raisins
- ½ cup candied fruit
- ½ teaspoon grated lemon rind
- 5 cups flour

Glaze

- 1 cup powdered sugar
- 2–4 tablespoons water

Mix yeast in warm water until dissolved. Add remaining ingredients, slowly adding flour until dough can be handled. You may not need all 5 cups. Knead dough on a floured board until smooth and elastic. Put dough in greased bowl. Cover and place in warm area—let rise until doubled in size , about 1 to 1½ hours. When risen, punch dough down and divide into 2 loaves. Place each loaf in a greased 3-lb. coffee can and allow to rise again about 45 minutes or until doubled in size. Bake 40 to 45 minutes at 375°. Cool, remove from cans and pour glaze over the top. To make the glaze, stir 2 tablespoons water with sugar. Add water a little at a time until creamy.

My Day With Anka

Nan Ferring Nelson • Illustrated by Bill Farnsworth
Lothrop, Lee & Shepard, 1996

On Thursdays Karrie smells the warm kolaches before she gets out of bed. She knows she'll spend the day with Anka, an elderly immigrant woman who shares tales of her travels from the Old Country as she cleans and cooks for Karrie's family. This is a warm story of a special friendship. *(all ages)*

Kolaches

- 1 cup warm water
- 1 cup warm milk
- 2 pkgs. yeast
- ⅓ cup butter, melted
- ¼ cup honey
- 1 teaspoon salt
- 2 eggs, well beaten
- ¼ teaspoon nutmeg
- ¼ teaspoon cinnamon
- grated peel from 1 lemon
- 1 teaspoon lemon juice
- 8½ cups flour
- 1 jar apricot jelly

Combine water and milk in a bowl. Add yeast and stir gently until dissolved. Add melted butter, honey, eggs, salt, peel of lemon and lemon juice. Beat in 3 to 4 cups of flour until smooth. Continue to add flour until a stiff dough is formed. Knead dough on a floured cutting board about 10 minutes, or until smooth. Place in an oiled bowl and let rise about an hour, or until dough doubles in size. When risen, place dough on floured board and punch down. Let dough sit about 15 minutes. Break off pieces of dough about the size of a golf ball. Roll into balls and put on a greased cookie sheet. Push a small dent in the top of the ball with your thumb and fill it with apricot jelly. Brush dough with melted butter, let rise 20 minutes. Bake for 15 to 20 minutes at 375°. Serve warm or cooled.

American Too

Elisa Barone • Illustrated by Ted Lewin
Lothrop, Lee & Shepard, 1996

Based on a true story about Rosie's arrival in the U.S. from Italy, much Italian American culture is shared. This is an excellent book to use when discussing immigration and the melting pot. In addition to the recipes below you can also have the children try lemon ice or chocolate gelato. Both of these delicious Italian desserts should be available in gourmet food stores or frozen food areas in grocery stores. *(all ages)*

Biscotti and Warm Milk

The easiest way to get biscotti is to go to a coffee shop and buy them. If you are more adventurous, you can make the recipe that follows:

- 2 cups flour
- 2 teaspoons baking powder
- ⅛ teaspoon salt
- 1½ teaspoons cinnamon
- ½ cup unsalted butter, softened

- ½ cup brown sugar, firmly packed
- ½ cup sugar
- 2 eggs
- 1 cup walnuts
- 1 cup chocolate chips

Combine dry ingredients and butter. Beat on high until fluffy. Add eggs one at a time and beat after each one. Add walnuts and chocolate chips and mix on low. Stir in dry ingredients until combined. Do not over mix. Divide dough in half and shape each piece into 3 inch wide by ¾ inch "loaves." Bake on a cookie sheet at 325° about 25 minutes or until firm. Remove from oven, let cool 5 minutes. Slice into ½ inch-wide slices. Return slices to cookie sheet with cut sides down. Bake until bottoms are brown. This should take about 10 minutes. Turn and bake second side. Cool. Store in an airtight container.

Zeppole

- 2 cups flour
- ¼ teaspoon salt
- 3 teaspoons baking powder
- ¼ teaspoon mace
- 2 eggs, beaten

- ¼ cup sugar
- ½ cup milk
- vegetable oil
- powdered sugar

Be sure all ingredients are at room temperature before starting. Mix flour, salt, mace and baking powder into a bowl. In a separate bowl beat eggs, add sugar and mix well. Stir in milk. Add to the dry ingredient mixture. Cover bowl and let sit for 20 minutes. Heat oil in a deep fryer to 370°. Be sure an adult works with the hot oil, not the children. Place a tablespoon of batter into hot oil and fry until golden, about 3 minutes. Drain on paper towels, sprinkle with powdered sugar and enjoy!

More recipes for this book on page 77.

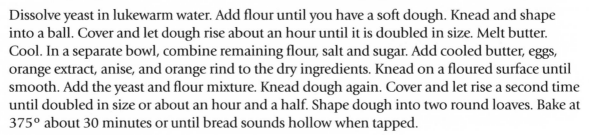

Day of the Dead

Tony Johnston • Illustrated by Jeannette Winter
See main entry on page 112

Pan de Muertos *(Bread of the Dead)*

- 1 pkg. yeast
- ½ cup water, lukewarm
- 3½ cups flour
- 1 teaspoon salt
- ½ cup sugar

- 1 stick butter
- 6 eggs, beaten
- 1 tablespoon orange extract
- 1 teaspoon ground anise
- rind of orange, grated

Dissolve yeast in lukewarm water. Add flour until you have a soft dough. Knead and shape into a ball. Cover and let dough rise about an hour until it is doubled in size. Melt butter. Cool. In a separate bowl, combine remaining flour, salt and sugar. Add cooled butter, eggs, orange extract, anise, and orange rind to the dry ingredients. Knead on a floured surface until smooth. Add the yeast and flour mixture. Knead dough again. Cover and let rise a second time until doubled in size or about an hour and a half. Shape dough into two round loaves. Bake at 375° about 30 minutes or until bread sounds hollow when tapped.

Pablo Remembers

George Ancona
See main entry on page 7

Pan de Muertos *(Bread of the Dead)*   See recipe above for pan de muertos.

Too Many Tamales

Gary Soto • Illustrated by Ed Martinez
Putnam, 1993

Maria helps mom make tortillas from masa. Mother takes off her diamond ring while she kneads the masa and Maria decides to slip the ring on "just for a minute." When the ring slips off, Maria worries that it slipped off in the dough and that her younger cousin swallowed it when he ate the tortillas. When making these tortillas make sure all hands are clean and all jewelry is removed. *(all ages)*

Tortillas

- 2½ cups masa harina (corn flour)*
- ½ teaspoon salt
- 1½ cups water

Combine flour and salt. Add 1 cup of lukewarm water and stir well. Knead dough on floured board, adding more dough if needed. The dough should not be sticky. Divide the dough into 12 to 15 small balls. Between pieces of waxed paper, roll each ball until it is about 4 inches in diameter. Cook each tortilla individually in a hot frying pan until brown and warm (about 2 minutes). Turn and repeat on flip side.

*Masa harina can be found in the grocery store with white flour.

More recipes for this book on page 77.

The Tortilla Factory

Gary Paulsen • Illustrated Ruth Wright Paulsen
Harcourt Brace, 1995

Using simple text, Gary Paulsen poetically describes how a tortilla is made from planting the seed, to harvesting the corn, to the tortilla factory where works "push the dough, squeeze the dough, flatten the dough" to make the tortillas. The finished tortillas are eaten to give strength to the hands that work the soil to plant the seed and the cycle begins again. *(ps, pm)*

Handmade Tortillas

To get the full effect of this book, it is imperative that you make tortillas from scratch. See above recipe for handmade tortillas. Eat the tortillas plain or fill with this bean filling on page 81.

Red Bird

Barbara Mitchell • Illustrated by Todd L. W.Doney
Lothrop, Lee & Shepard, 1996

Katie, whose Nanticoke name is Red Bird, and her mom and dad leave the city for the Nanticoke pow-wow in the country. Red Bird meets her aunts, uncles and cousins for the annual ceremony. Fry bread and spicy beans are eaten at this celebratory event. *(pm, in)*

Fry Bread

- 2 cups flour
- 1 teaspoon salt
- 2 teaspoons baking powder
- 2 tablespoons oil
- ⅔ cup warm water
- cooking oil

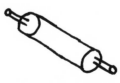

Mix dry ingredients together. Add shortening until mixture looks like fine crumbs. Add water a spoonful at a time, mixing with fork until dough forms a ball. Cover bowl with towel and refrigerate a half hour. In a large pot, heat 1 inch of oil. Divide dough into 10 to 12 pieces. On a lightly floured surface, flatten each piece into a 6-inch circle. Fry dough on each side until browned. Drain fry bread on a paper towel or napkin. Serve warm.

More recipes for this book on page 80.

The Green Gourd

C.W. Hunter • Illustrated Tony Griego
Putnam, 1992

In this North Carolina folktale, a little old woman fails to listen to the warning: Never pick a green gourd "afore its ripe or it'll witch ye sure." After she ignores this warning, trouble starts a brewin'. The green gourd chases her down, continually trying to "frump" her, until a young boy comes to her rescue. She celebrates by fixing homemade butter and biscuits. In the end she has learned her lesson. *(all ages)*

Biscuits

- 2½ cups self-rising flour
- 1½ cups milk
- 5 tablespoons mayonnaise

Combine flour, milk and mayonnaise. Drop mixture on a well-greased cookie sheet. Bake at 450° for 12 to 15 minutes or until golden brown. Makes 27 biscuits.

Homemade Butter   For homemade butter recipe, see page 33.

An Angel for Solomon Singer

Cynthia Rylant • Illustrated by Peter Catalanottl
Orchard Books, 1992

Solomon Singer lives in New York City in a hotel for men. He hates New York and wanders the streets often. One night he wanders into the Westway Cafe, a place where all your dreams come true. Solomon Singer imagines that he is back in Indiana and can see warm yellow lights coming from the house where he lived as a boy. Solomon Singer feels he has finally found a place he loves to be and where he does not feel lonely. This mysterious book raises many discussion questions. *(all ages)*

Biscuits

- 1 cup biscuit mix
- ½ cup whole wheat
- ¼ cup dry milk
- water
- vegetable oil

Combine all ingredients except oil. Add just enough water to the dry ingredients to make a sticky dough. Heat oil in a skillet. Drop dough into oil and fry until golden brown. Serve warm.

More recipes for this book on pages 67 and 110.

Jam Day

Barbara M. Josse • Illustrated by Emily Arnold McCully
Harper and Row, 1987

One morning when Ben and his mother are visiting Grandma and Grandpap, Grandma announces that it's Jam Day! The family goes strawberry picking and returns to make jam and Grandpap's world-famous biscuit recipe. A recipe for strawberry jam is under *Jamberry* on page 34. *(ps, pm)*

Biscuits

- 2 cups flour
- 4 teaspoons baking powder
- ½ teaspoon salt
- 2 tablespoons sugar
- ½ teaspoon cream of tartar
- ½ cup shortening
- ⅔ cup milk
- 1 egg, unbeaten

Sift flour, baking powder, salt, sugar, and cream of tartar into a bowl. Add shortening and blend until it has a cornmeal-like consistency. Slowly pour milk into the flour mixture. Add egg and stir to a stiff dough. Knead 5 times. Roll dough out to ½ inch thickness. Cut with 1½-inch cookie cutter. Bake for 10 to 15 minutes at 450°.

The Bun

Marcia Brown
Harcourt Brace Jovanovich, 1972

This Russian tale is another of the many books that utilize the theme of the "Gingerbread Man." A little old woman makes a bun for a little old man. When the bun is set in the window, he begins to roll away. He is chased by the little old man and woman and several animals until, like the gingerbread man, he is tricked by the sly old fox. *(all ages)*

Buns

- 4 cups self-rising flour
- ¼ cup sugar
- 1 pkg. yeast
- 1 egg, well beaten
- ¾ stick melted butter
- 2 cups warm water

Mix all ingredients together. Grease muffin tins and fill them half full. Let rise. Bake for 20 minutes at 375°. Makes about 30 buns.

The Funny Little Woman

Retold by Arlene Mosel • Illustrated by Blair Lent
E. P. Dutton, 1972 ★ Caldecott Award Winner

The funny little woman makes a rice dumpling that falls down a hole into a strange underworld—the home of the wicked oni. Will she be able to escape from him? *(all ages)*

Rice Dumplings

- 1 cup flour
- 2 teaspoons baking powder
- ¼ teaspoon salt
- 2 tablespoons oil
- ½ cup milk
- 1 cup white rice, cooked
- 1 can chicken broth

Combine dry ingredients, then mix in oil, milk and rice. Heat chicken broth in a pot. Shape dumplings and drop into boiling chicken broth. Cover and cook 15 minutes. Do not lift the cover while dumplings are steaming.

Davy Dumpling
Traditional Mother Goose

Davy Davy Dumpling,
Boil him in a pot;
Sugar him and butter him,
Eat him while he's hot.

Dumplings

- 2 cups flour
- 3½ teaspoons baking powder
- ½ cup milk
- ½ teaspoon salt
- 2 cans chicken broth

Combine flour, baking powder, milk, and salt; mix well. Heat the chicken broth until it boils. Drop dumplings by the spoonful into broth. Turn heat down to medium. Put lid on pot and cook dumplings for 15 minutes.

This Is the Way We Eat Our Lunch
Edith Bauer • Illustrated by Steve Bjorkman
See main entry on page 1

Pretzels (soft)

- 1 pkg. dry yeast
- 1½ cups warm water
- 4 cups flour
- ¾ teaspoon salt
- 1 egg white
- coarse salt

Dissolve yeast in warm water. In a separate bowl, combine dry ingredients. Add to yeast mixture and blend well. On a floured board, knead dough for about 5 minutes. Divide dough into 18 balls. Roll the balls into long snakes about ½ inch around. Twist into pretzel shapes or have children shape them into their initials. Place on greased cooked sheets. Beat egg white and brush over pretzels. Sprinkle with coarse salt. Bake at 400° for 15 minutes or until golden.

Walter the Baker
Eric Carle
Simon & Schuster, 1972 — Rereleased 1995

Walter the Baker is the best baker in town. Even the Duke and Duchess who rule over Duchy love his rolls. One day when Walter's cat spills his milk, Walter substitutes water for the milk called for in the recipe. His rolls turn out hard as stones. The Duke threatens to banish Walter unless he can "invent a roll through which the rising sun can shine three times." The roll must also be made from one piece of dough and taste good too! Walter tries to create such a roll and almost gives up when he accidentally creates a pretzel. Maybe you will enjoy these pretzels as much as the townsfolk enjoyed the ones made by Walter. *(ps, pm)*

Pretzels

- 1 pkg. dry yeast
- 1½ cups warm water
- 1 teaspoon salt
- ¾ tablespoon sugar

- 4 cups flour
- 1 egg, beaten
- coarse salt

Dissolve yeast in warm water. Add sugar and salt. Add flour to mixture. Knead until smooth. Divide dough into small balls. Roll balls into long ropes; twist into pretzel shapes where "the rising sun can rise three times." Put on cookie sheet, brush with beaten egg and sprinkle with coarse salt. Bake for 10 to 15 minutes at 425°.

An Early American Christmas

Tomie dePaola
Holiday House, 1987

This book is full of Christmas foods and activities from colonial times for your class to try. You can use the tips for stringing popcorn or perhaps you'll want to cook up some pretzels. *(all ages)*

Pretzels

- 1 pkg. quick-rise dry yeast
- ¾ cup warm water
- 1½ teaspoons salt
- 1 tablespoon sugar

- 1½–3 cups flour
- egg white
- coarse salt

Combine water and yeast. When the yeast is dissolved, add the salt and sugar. Mix in 2 cups of flour. Add more flour if needed until the dough loses its stickiness. Knead dough until smooth (about 5 to 10 minutes). Let dough rise 30 to 40 minutes.

After the dough rises, give each child a piece about the size of a 2-inch ball. Roll into a rope and twist into a pretzel shape. Place on greased cookie sheets. Brush with egg white and sprinkle with coarse salt. Bake 12 to 15 minutes at 425°.

Hot Cross Buns

Traditional Mother Goose

Hot cross buns, hot cross buns,
One a penny, two a penny,
Hot cross buns.

Give them to your daughters,
Give them to your sons;
One a penny, two a penny,
Hot cross buns.

Hot Cross Buns

- 3½–4 cups flour
- 2 pkgs. quick-rise yeast
- 2 teaspoons cinnamon
- ½ cup oil
- ¾ cup milk
- frosting
- ½ teaspoon salt
- 3 eggs
- ⅔ cup raisins
- 1 egg white, beaten
- ⅓ cup sugar

Combine 2 cups of the flour with yeast and cinnamon. Heat oil, milk, sugar, and salt until it is 115° on a candy thermometer. Add the milk mixture to the dry ingredients. Add eggs and beat at a low speed with an electric mixer for about 1 minute. Stir in the raisins. Add enough flour to make a soft dough. Place in a greased bowl; cover and let rise until dough doubles in size. Punch down, cover, and let rise 5 to 10 more minutes.

Divide dough into 16 balls. Put on greased cookie sheet about 1½ inches apart. Cover and let rise again until doubled. With a knife, cut an "X" or cross on each bun. Brush each with beaten egg white. Bake for 12 to 15 minutes at 375°. Using a tube of frosting, frost an "X" or cross on each bun.

If You Give a Moose a Muffin

Laura Joffe Numeroff • Illustrated by Felicia Bond
HarperCollins, 1991

Much like her previous book, *If You Give a Mouse a Cookie*, this whimsical story describes the humorous events that could occur if you were to give a moose a muffin—ending exactly where the story began. *(ps, pm)*

Muffins

- 2 cups apples, finely chopped
- ½ cup sugar
- 1 banana, mashed
- 1 egg, beaten
- 1 cup and 1 tablespoon flour
- 1 teaspoon salt
- 1 teaspoon cinnamon
- 1 teaspoon baking powder

Combine apples, banana and sugar together in a mixing bowl. Add egg. Mix dry ingredients together in a separate bowl. Add to apples and banana mixture. Grease muffin tins, or use cupcake liners—fill ½ to ⅔ full. Bake for 20 minutes at 350°.

The Muffin Man

Traditional Mother Goose

Oh, do you know the muffin man,
The muffin man, the muffin man?
Oh, do you know the muffin man
Who lives on Drury Lane?

Muffins

- 2 cups biscuit mix
- 2 tablespoons sugar
- 1 egg
- ¾ cup milk

Combine the above ingredients and beat vigorously for half a minute. Grease muffin tins. Fill tins ⅔ full. Bake at 400° for 15 minutes.

Topping

- 1 cup sugar
- 1 teaspoon cinnamon
- 1 stick butter or margarine

Combine sugar and cinnamon. Melt butter. When muffins are done, dip the top in the melted butter and roll in sugar mixture.

Molly and Grandpa

Sally G. Ward
Scholastic, 1986

As Grandpa looks for the recipe for blueberry muffins, Molly goes in the kitchen to get started. What is taking Grandpa so long? Molly starts without him. Wait until you see what happens in the kitchen! *(ps, pm)*

You can buy a box of blueberry muffins where you find the cake mixes, or you can use the easy recipe below.

Blueberry Muffins

- 2 cups flour
- ¼ cup sugar
- ½ teaspoon salt
- 1 tablespoon baking powder
- 1 cup milk
- ¼ cup cooking oil
- 2 eggs, lightly beaten
- 1 cup blueberries

Combine the dry ingredients. Mix in enough milk to make a stiff dough—you might not need the entire cup. Stir in the oil, eggs, and blueberries. Fill muffin cups ⅔ full. If you do not use cupcake paper, be sure to grease the muffin trays. Bake at 400° for 30 minutes. Makes approximately 1 dozen average-sized muffins or 2 dozen small muffins.

Loose Tooth

Steven Kroll • Illustrated by Tricia Tusa
Holiday House, 1984

Flapper and Fangs are twin bats and do everything together until Fang loses a tooth. Flapper feels like everyone now ignores him. He steals Fang's tooth and accidentally drops it in the muffin batter that Mom is making. When you bake the muffins on the next page, you might add a peanut in the batter. The children will have to chew carefully until the peanut is found! *(ps, pm)*

Muffins

- 1¼ cups flour
- 1 tablespoon baking powder
- 1¼ teaspoons salt
- 2 tablespoons sugar
- 1 cup bran cereal
- 1 cup milk
- 3 tablespoons cooking oil
- 1 egg
- 1 large peanut

Stir together the flour, baking powder, salt, and sugar. In a separate bowl, combine the cereal and milk; let stand for about 2 minutes. Add oil and egg; beat well. Add the dry ingredients and peanut to the egg mixture and stir only until combined. Do not over stir. Pour batter into greased muffin cups or muffin papers until ⅔ full. Bake 20 to 25 minutes at 400°. Makes about 12 regular-size muffins.

Homer Price

Robert McCloskey
Viking, 1943

Homer Price has many humorous adventures, the most famous being the chapter entitled "Doughnuts." *(pm, in)*

Doughnuts

- refrigerator biscuits
- cooking oil
- powdered sugar

Using a bottle cap or thimble, let the students cut a hole from the center of a biscuit. Heat 1 inch of oil in electric skillet set at 350°. An adult should fry the doughnuts because of the hot oil. Fry biscuits and cutout holes in oil about 1 minute on each side or until browned. Add more oil as needed to complete all the doughnuts. Drain oil from doughnuts by placing them on paper towels. Roll in powdered sugar or eat plain.

Old Witch Rescues Halloween

Wende and Harry Devlin
Four Winds, 1972

Mean old Mr. Butterbean, who is always chasing children away, has decided there will be no Halloween. Since he owns most of the town of Oldswick, Nicky knows everyone usually listens to whatever he says! Nicky calls on Old Witch to help. Will she be able to save Halloween? *(all ages)*

Sugar Doughnuts

After reading the story, serve sugar doughnuts and apple cider like the children have at the party. If your class would like to make doughnuts, refer to the recipe listed with *Homer Price* above.

Spreads, Sauces

Pancakes for Breakfast

Tomie dePaola
Harcourt Brace Jovanovich, 1978

You'll find a recipe for pancakes in this wordless book. In addition to making pancakes, the little old lady goes to the chicken house to fetch her eggs, milks the cow, churns her butter, and purchases maple syrup from a man who taps his own trees.

If you can arrange to visit a farm to buy eggs and milk or go to a maple sugaring, it would really help your students to live the experiences in *Pancakes for Breakfast*. Be sure to make pancakes from the recipe in the book and serve them up with some homemade butter. *(all ages)*

Homemade Butter

- 2 cartons heavy cream
- 5–6 jars with lids; baby food jars work well

Divide the cream evenly among the jars. Have your students sit in a circle and distribute the jars to every fifth or sixth child. Let each student shake the jar 50 or 60 times before passing it to the next child. If you sing a song and pass the jars after the song each time, the task will pass more quickly. It takes about 20 to 40 minutes, depending on the temperature and age of the cream, before the butter separates from the buttermilk. If you use several jars as suggested, the children will get a chance to shake the jar more often than if you just use one jar.

Salt the butter slightly before serving, if desired. Use the butter on pancakes, as in the book, or spread it on saltine crackers. (See the recipe for pancakes listed with *Johnny-Cake* on page 11.)

You might want to point out the difference in color between homemade butter and butter purchased at the grocery store. You can add some yellow food coloring to show that the color does not change the taste.

Brown Cow, Green Grass, Yellow Mellow Sun

Ellen Jackson • Illustrated by Victoria Raymond
Hyperion, 1995

Simple text explains how the yellow sun warms the earth, how a brown cow eats green grass and gives milk, and how a child and his granny churn the milk into butter. *(ps, pm)*

Yellow Mellow Butter

Author Ellen Jackson provides recipes for Big Brown Pancakes and Yellow Mellow Butter at the end of her story. You may want to use this recipe for butter or try the one above. See page 10 for a pancake recipe to have with this fresh butter.

Peanut Butter and Jelly

Illustrated by Nadine Bernard Westcott
E. P. Dutton, 1987

A version of this play rhyme is also a song. It's a humorous song about making peanut butter and jelly. The recipe below is for making peanut butter. If you also wish to make jelly, see the recipe on page 35 for *Blueberries for Sal*. *(all ages as song)*

Peanut Butter

- 1 jar or bag of shelled peanuts
- cooking oil

Place ¼ cup of peanuts in a blender at a time. Turn blender on high and blend for 10 to 15 seconds. If the peanuts need to be crushed more, repeat for 10 to 15 more seconds. This keeps the motor from overworking. When blended, add another ¼ cup of peanuts to the blender. Add a little oil if it looks like the peanut butter is dry. Some peanuts are very oily and you do not need much oil. Other peanuts are drier and more oil will be needed. Add enough oil to moisten the peanut butter to a spreadable consistency.

Jamberry

Bruce Degen
Harper and Row, 1983

This book is written in rhyme, celebrating a variety of berries—raspberries, blueberries, strawberries, and even a brassberry band. You can't help but want to make jam! *(ps, pm)*

Strawberry Jam

- 2 pints strawberries
- 4 cups sugar
- 3 ozs. liquid fruit pectin
- 2 tablespoons lemon juice

Using a potato masher, mash 1 pint of strawberries at a time until you have 2 cups of mashed berries. Add sugar and mix well. Let stand 10 minutes. In another bowl, mix lemon juice and liquid pectin. Add this to the strawberries. Stir for 3 to 4 minutes, mixing well. Fill sterilized baby food jars. Let jam set for 24 hours at room temperature. Store in refrigerator or freezer.

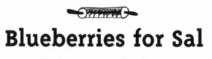

Blueberries for Sal

Robert McCloskey
Viking, 1948 ★ Caldecott Honor Book

If possible, take your class blueberry picking before making blueberry jam just like Little Sal and her mother. *(ps, pm)*

Blueberry Jam

- 3 pints blueberries
- 3 tablespoons lemon juice
- 7 cups sugar
- 2 pouches liquid fruit pectin

Wash berries and remove stems. Using a potato masher, crush berries in a large bowl. Measure 4½ cups mashed berries. If you do not have 4½ cups, add water until you have this amount.

Combine blueberries and lemon juice in a cooking pot. Stir in sugar. Bring to a full rolling boil. Boil for 1 minute, stirring constantly. Remove from heat. Stir in pectin. Skim off foam. Put into sterilized baby food jars.

A Bear Called Paddington

Michael Bond
Dell, 1968

In the Paddington Bear series, Paddington has a real fondness for marmalade. *(all ages)*

Marmalade

- 3 oranges
- 2 lemons
- 10 cups water
- 8 cups sugar

Thoroughly wash the rinds on all fruit. Cut into quarters, remove seeds, and soak in 10 cups of water overnight. Remove fruit from water, reserving water. Cut oranges and lemons into fine pieces. Put fruit pieces back in water and boil for 1 hour. Add sugar. Boil until a candy thermometer reaches 222°. Pour into sterilized baby food jars.

Famous Seaweed Soup

Antoinette Truglio Martin • Illustrated by Nadine Bernard Westcott
Albert Whitman, 1993

When Sara and her family go to the beach, Sara wants help making her famous seaweed soup. Since everyone in her family is too busy to help, she makes her soup all by herself. She adds water, feathers, beach glass and other beach treasures to her pretend soup. Young children will immediately notice the familiar pattern from *The Little Red Hen*. *(ps, pm)*

Jelly Sandwiches

Most children probably think of grape jelly when they think about jelly sandwiches. Perhaps you will want to share other types of jelly with your class, such as: strawberry, logan berry, raspberry, mint and others. If you think you want to add more new experiences, try a variety of breads to make your sandwiches with too—not just white, soft bread. Try whole wheat, sprouted wheat, sour dough, oatmeal, pumpernickel, rye or 7-grain.

More recipes for this book on page 49.

Bread and Jam for Frances

Russell Hoban • Illustrated by Lillian Hoban
Harper and Row, 1964

Frances does not want to eat anything but bread and jam for breakfast, lunch, and dinner. Her family tries to get her to taste some other foods but to no avail. How do her parents finally solve this problem? *(ps, pm)*

Bread and Jam

- 1 to 2 loaves of bread
- 1 jar grape jam

Each child spreads about a tablespoon of jam on his or her bread. This can be eaten as an open-face sandwich, or the child can use 2 pieces of bread for a jam sandwich.

The Honey Makers

Gail Gibbons
Morrow Junior Books, 1997

Another of Gail Gibbon's nonfiction books, this one explains the life cycle of honey bees and how honey is made. It's a good book to read with *A Beekeeper's Year* (page 21). *(pm, in)*

Honey

At the end *The Honey Makers*, a family is seen spreading honey on a piece of bread. Provide bread and honey for the children, or bake a loaf of bread and serve it warm with honey from a local honey farm.

Cranberries

William Jaspersohn
Houghton Mifflin, 1991

This is an excellent book to share with your class during November when thoughts are on turkeys and cranberries. Colorful photographs accompany the text of this nonfiction book about cranberry bogs and how cranberries are harvested. Be sure to make enough cranberry sauce so that the children can bring home a small jar to share with their families for Thanksgiving. *(pm, in)*

Cranberry Sauce

- 1 bag fresh cranberries
- 1 cup sugar
- 1 cup water

Combine all ingredients in a sauce pan. Bring to a boil. Turn down the heat and simmer until cranberries pop, about 15 to 25 minutes. As the sauce cools, it thickens. One bag of fresh cranberries makes enough to fill about 5 small baby food jars.

Hoang Anh
A Vietnamese American Boy
Diane Hoyt-Goldsmith • Photographs by Lawrence Migdale
Holiday House, 1992

This book is a photo essay about Hoang Anh, a Vietnamese boy living in California. Hoang describes Vietnamese culture and customs, and his daily life in the United States. *(pm, in)*

Fresh Cucumbers dipped in Nuoc Nam

Nuoc Mam (*Nook Nam*) is a very popular spicy fish sauce served in Viet Nam, like ketchup is used in the U.S. or soy sauce is used in China. It is made from anchovies, or other fish, and salt that ferment in barrels for about nine months. The first drawing from the finished sauce is the best and most expensive. This is the sauce used most at the table. The second and third draining are of a lower quality and are best used for cooking. Look for fish sauce in oriental markets. *Ca Com* on the label indicates that only anchovies were used to make the sauce, producing a higher quality for table use.

Nuoc Nam

If you want to make this sauce rather than buy it, the recipe is below. Due to the burning effect of chilies, it is advised that an adult make the sauce and have the children taste it instead of having the children come in contact with hot chilies during the preparation.

- 1–2 red chilies
- 1 clove garlic
- ¾ teaspoon sugar
- 1 fresh lemon
- 1 tablespoon vinegar
- 1 tablespoon water
- 3½ tablespoons fish sauce

Remove seeds and membrane from chilies. Put all ingredients in blender and blend well. Have the children wash and slice cucumbers to dip in this sauce for a Vietnamese treat.

More recipes for this book on page 60.

Little Miss Muffet
Traditional Mother Goose

Little Miss Muffet
Sat on a tuffet,
Eating her curds and whey.
Along came a spider
And sat down beside her,
And frightened Miss Muffet away.

Curds and Whey
- 2 cups milk
- salt
- 1½ tablespoons vinegar

Heat the milk until it just starts to boil. Remove from heat. Add vinegar and stir constantly until curds start to form. Separate the curds from the liquid. This liquid is the whey. Taste a small amount of curds on bread or your favorite cracker. Add a pinch of salt if desired.

Sandwiches, Tacos

Cat and Dog

Peta Coplans
Viking, 1995

When Dog walks down the beach and finds Cat, Cat won't share his picnic lunch. Dog tricks Cat by asking him to count things on the beach, eating part of Cat's picnic each time Cat turns to count the objects. Listed below are a variety of foods packed in Cat's lunch, most of which need no preparation. An easy cucumber sandwich would be fun to make using cookie cutters to shape the bread.

Cat's lunch includes: strawberries, chips, glazed doughnuts, salty crackers, raisins, cupcakes, tiny fish and tomatoes. Perhaps you could have these available for a luncheon or picnic. *(ps, pm)*

Cucumber Sandwiches

- 2–3 slices bread per child
- cream cheese
- 2–3 cucumbers
- paprika
- variety of cookie cutter

Each child uses cookie cutter of choice to cut bread. Spread cream cheese on bread. Slice very thin cucumber pieces. Put a slice of cucumber on each slice of bread. Sprinkle with paprika.

Place open-faced sandwiches on a platter with a doily to make an elegant appetizer.

Sylvester and the Magic Pebble

William Steig
Simon & Schuster, 1969 ⭐ Caldecott Award Winner

Sylvester finds a red, round magic pebble and discovers his wishes all come true. When he's frightened by a lion, he wishes, without thinking, that he was a rock. Will he ever get changed back into a donkey? *(all ages)*

Alfalfa Sandwiches

On a picnic, while looking for Sylvester, his parents have some alfalfa sandwiches. You can buy alfalfa sprouts in the produce section of the grocery store or you can grow your own. Alfalfa sprouts are easy to grow. Buy alfalfa seeds at a health food store. Put 1 tablespoon of seeds in a mayonnaise jar. Cut 4 or 5 pieces of cheesecloth large enough to fit over the top of the jar. Secure the cheesecloth pieces over the opening with a rubber band. Run water in the jar and drain through the cheesecloth. Rinse the seeds daily and keep the jar in the sun. They should sprout in about five to seven days.

Make sandwiches by placing a small bunch of sprouts and a tablespoon of plain yogurt on half a piece of pita or pocket bread.

Food Fight
Edited and illustrated by Michael J. Rosen
Harcourt Brace, 1996

Michael Rosen has chosen food-related poems by such poets as Jack Prelutsky, J. Patrick Lewis and Crescent Dragonwagon. Included below is a recipe to be made after reading "Sunday O Sunday" by Mimi Brodsky Chenfeld. *(pm, in)*

"Sunday O Sunday" Grilled Cheese

Traditional grilled cheese sandwiches can be made after reading this poem. Making these sandwiches with an iron puts a fun twist on a common sandwich. Make a grilled cheese sandwich with an iron??? *Yes!*

For each child you will need:

- 2 pieces of bread
- 1 slice of cheese
- 1 tablespoon butter
- 1 piece of aluminum foil, large enough to wrap sandwich

Each child butters both slices of bread. Make a sandwich, slipping cheese between bread leaving buttered sides out. Wrap sandwich in one layer of foil. Cut off extra foil rather than wrapping any extra foil around sandwich. An adult needs to work with the iron: Heat iron on cotton setting. Hold the iron on each side of the foil-wrapped cheese sandwich until butter and cheese melt and sandwich becomes golden brown, about 1 to 2 minutes on each side.

More recipes for this book on page 48.

Little Red Riding Hood
Retold and illustrated by Trina Schart Hyman
Holiday House, 1983 ★ Caldecott Honor Book

In this beautifully illustrated version of the well-known fairy tale, Little Red Riding Hood takes sweet butter, bread, and wine to grandmother's house. *(all ages)*

Bread and Sweet Butter

Let each child butter his or her own piece of bread to eat after reading this book together. If you don't want to use store-bought bread and butter, you can find the recipe for butter under *Pancakes for Breakfast* on page 33, and for homemade bread under *The Little Red Hen* on page 17.

Little Tommy Tucker
Traditional Mother Goose

Little Tommy Tucker
Sings for his supper.
What shall we give him?
White bread and butter.

Bread and Butter

Buy 1 or 2 loaves of white bread and a tub of butter (not margarine). Allow the children to butter their own pieces of bread. If you are talking about shapes, let them cut their bread into two rectangles or triangles. This is also a good way to teach them about the concept "one-half."

You might want to provide both salted and unsalted butter so your students can taste the difference between the two. If you want to make your own butter, see the recipe listed under *Pancakes for Breakfast* (page 33). To make your own bread, see the bread recipe with *The Little Red Hen* on page 17.

Lunch with Milly
Jeanne Modesitt • Illustrated by Robin Spowart
Bridgewater, 1995

Milly and her friend eat peanut butter, banana, and sunflower seed sandwiches together before flying out the window in search of dessert. They meet several animals who give them strawberries, a jar of lemons and fresh mint leaves. After flying back home they prepare a "lovely, wonderful, splendid dessert."

Lunch with Milly includes a recipe for "Strawberries with Lemon and Mint" that you can prepare. You may also want to make the sandwiches that Milly and her friend enjoy. *(ps, pm)*

Peanut Butter, Banana and Sunflower Seed Sandwich

For each sandwich you will need:

- 2 pieces of bread
- ½ banana
- 1 tablespoon sunflower seeds
- peanut butter

Spread peanut butter on each slice of bread. Slice the ½ banana, placing slices on one of the pieces of bread. Sprinkle with sunflower seeds.

The Hungry Little Boy
Joan W. Blos • Illustrated by Dena Schutzer
Simon & Schuster, 1995

On a rainy day, a grandmother fixes lunch for a hungry little boy before the sun shines and they go out to play. This is a simple story perfect for preschool listeners. *(ps)*

Peanut Butter Sandwich

Serve with 4 pieces of carrot, 3 cookies, 1 apple and a glass of milk—just like in the book! Children can make their own sandwiches, clean the carrots, count out 3 cookies and pour their own milk.

Ernest and Celestine's Picnic

Gabrielle Vincent
Greenwillow, 1982

Ernest and Celestine plan to go on the best picnic ever. But when they wake up in the morning, it is raining. Celestine is very disappointed. They decide to take their picnic of sandwiches and tea, build a rain shelter, and pretend the sun is shining. *(ps, pm)*

Sandwiches and Tea

Have each student make a honey or Swiss cheese sandwich just like Ernest and Celestine do. And don't forget the pot of tea. This would be a great book and activity to share on a rainy day or if a picnic you plan gets rained out. Have a picnic in the rain just like Ernest and Celestine!

My Kitchen

Harlow Rockwell
Greenwillow, 1980

A child takes the reader on a tour through his kitchen, explaining how he makes his lunch of chicken noodle soup, a peanut butter sandwich, and milk. *(ps)*

Soup and Sandwich

- bread
- peanut butter
- milk
- 2 large cans of chicken noodle soup

Each child makes his or her own peanut butter sandwich and pours a glass of milk. Prepare the soup according to the directions on the can.

Be-Bop-a-Do-Walk

Sheila Hamanaka
Simon & Schuster, 1995

Pack up your jelly sandwiches along with Emi, her father, and her friend Martha, as you read about the sights they visit in New York City. Before your visit is complete you may also wish to make the origami boats, hats and cranes that are mentioned in the story. *(all ages)*

Jelly Sandwiches

For each child you will need:

- 2 slices bread
- 1 tablespoon jelly

Each child can make their own sandwich to eat while you show them some simple origami hats, boats and paper cranes.

This Is the Way We Eat Our Lunch
Edith Bauer • Illustrated by Steve Bjorkman
See main entry on page 1

Tacos

- 2 ½ cups diced chicken, or
- 1½ lbs cooked hamburger
- 1½ tablespoons vegetable oil
- 1 onion, chopped
- 1 small green pepper, chopped
- 1 teaspoon chili powder, or taco seasoning

- 1 can tomato sauce
- 1 jar mild taco sauce
- lettuce, shredded
- tomatoes, chopped
- grated cheese
- tortillas or taco shells

Saute green pepper and onion in oil in a skillet. Add chicken, salt and pepper, seasoning, tomato sauce, and half jar of taco sauce. Cook for 15 minutes, stirring occasionally. Spoon meat mixture into tortillas or taco shells. Add choice of toppings.

Three Stalks of Corn
Leo Politi
Charles Scribner's, 1976

Angelica lives with her grandmother in California in an area called "Barrio de Picoviejo," where there are many people of Mexican descent. Angelica learns about corn and its importance to the Mexican culture. Every bit of the corn is precious, no part is thrown away, not even the husk. Several foods are mentioned and the children even cook at school! Recipes for tacos and enchiladas are included in the book. You may even want to grind corn to make cornmeal for tortillas as they do in the story. *(all ages)*

Enchiladas

- 1 cup vegetable oil
- 8 tortillas
- 1 onion, finely chopped

- ½ pound cheese
- salsa

Heat oil in skillet. Fry tortilla until tender; this should just take a few seconds. Spread a little salsa on tortilla. Sprinkle on cheese and onions. Roll up and place in a baking dish with opening side down. Continue with each tortilla. Add some salsa to bottom of pan and over enchiladas. Top with cheese. Bake at 325° for 15 to 20 minutes.

More recipes for this book on page 113.

🍲 Chili, Soups, Stews 🍲

Chicken Soup with Rice

Maurice Sendak
Harper and Row, 1962

Make it once, make it twice, make some chicken soup with rice! Written in rhyme, this book includes a special rhyme for each month of the year. Try to find a copy of the miniature version from The Nutshell Library. For the chicken soup, you can heat several cans of chicken soup with rice or make the recipe below. *(ps, pm)*

Chicken Soup with Rice

- 8 cups seasoned chicken broth
- 1 cup chopped celery
- ½ cup rice

Heat broth; add celery and cook until tender. Add rice and cook until fluffy. If you want to add more vegetables, such as carrots and onions, or spices such as bay leaves, add them when you put in the celery.

The Keeping Quilt

Patricia Polacco
See main entry on page 21

Chicken Soup

- 1 large chicken, quartered
- 5 carrots
- 3 onions
- 3 stalks celery
- 1 tomato
- 2 cloves garlic, minced
- 2 chicken bouillon cubes
- salt and pepper to taste

Place chicken pieces in large pan. Add water to cover chicken. Bring to a boil. Have the children chop the vegetables. Add chopped vegetables, garlic and bouillon to pot. Bring to a boil again. Reduce heat and simmer 2 to 3 hours. Cool. Remove meat from bones. Serve hot.

Watch Out for Chicken Feet in Your Soup

Tomie dePaola
Prentice Hall, 1974

Joey and his friend visit Joey's grandmother. Grandmother feeds the boys well and makes them each a bread doll. The bread doll recipe is included in the book. You might also wish to make spaghetti (see pages 58–59) or this chicken soup. Oh, and watch out for the chicken feet! *(ps, pm)*

Chicken Soup

- 2 onions, quartered
- 2–3 carrots, sliced
- 1–2 celery sticks, diced
- 1 whole chicken, or 1 pkg. of chicken parts
- 3–4 chicken flavor bouillon cubes
- 1 bay leaf

Put all the ingredients in a pot. Cover with water. Heat to a boil and then simmer about 1½ hours or until chicken falls off the bone easily. Bone the chicken and throw away the bones. Return meat to soup and serve.

Growing Vegetable Soup

Lois Ehlert
Harcourt Brace Jovanovich, 1987

This colorful book is about planting and growing a vegetable garden. The pictures are bright and vivid. Make vegetable soup using the recipe included in the book or the one below. *(ps, pm)*

Vegetable Soup

- 1 onion, diced
- 1½ cups celery, sliced
- 2 potatoes, diced
- 3 fresh tomatoes, or 1 large can tomatoes
- 1½ teaspoons salt
- 1½ cups carrots, sliced
- 1 cup shredded cabbage

Put ingredients in a pot and cook until vegetables are tender. Add barley to thicken if desired.

George and Martha

James Marshall
Houghton Mifflin, 1972

George and Martha are hippos and very good friends. Martha loves to make split pea soup. She makes pot after pot of soup for George. George, unfortunately, hates split pea soup, but he doesn't know how to tell Martha. When she catches him pouring the soup into his shoes, he finally admits he hates split pea soup. They agree that honesty is the best way to keep a friend, and Martha admits she hates to eat the soup, too, she only likes to make it. They decide Martha will make chocolate chip cookies instead. *(ps, pm)*

Split Pea Soup

- 1 pkg. split green peas
- 1 onion, diced
- 1 potato, diced
- 3 carrots, diced
- ham bone, ham hocks, or Canadian bacon
- salt and pepper to taste

Soak the peas overnight. Drain off excess water. Add 1½ gallons of fresh water, onion, potato, carrots, and ham. Bring to a boil and simmer 1½ to 2 hours.

Stone Soup

Marcia Brown

Charles Scribner, 1947 ★ Caldecott Honor Book

Three hungry soldiers convince villagers to share their food by showing them how to make soup from a stone. This is a good meal for kids to make and share—along with the story—with another class. Have each child bring a vegetable to contribute to the stone soup. You can ask several children to bring the same vegetables so that everyone has a chance to contribute. *(all ages)*

Stone Soup

- 3 smooth, clean stones
- canned or fresh corn
- canned or fresh peas
- potatoes
- garlic
- carrots
- celery
- zucchini
- green beans
- onions
- fresh or canned tomatoes
- 1½ lbs. hamburger
- beef bouillon cubes

Have each child wash and chop the vegetable that he or she brought and put it into the soup pot. Brown the hamburger, garlic, and onions. Drain the meat and add to the vegetables. Add stones and water to cover. Dissolve 3 or 4 bouillon cubes and add to the soup mixture. Cook on medium heat until the potatoes and carrots are tender. Serve with crackers.

Nail Soup

Retold by Harve Zemach • Illustrated by Margot Zemach
Follett, 1964

Nail Soup is another version of *Stone Soup*, where a nail is used to make the soup instead of a stone.

Nail Soup

Use the recipe listed with *Stone Soup* above. Or open several cans of chunky-style vegetable soup and add a nail for "extra flavoring." Be sure to wash the nail before adding it to the soup, as some new nails have a light coating of oil to prevent rust.

Group Soup

Barbara Brenner • Illustrated by Lynn Munsinger
Viking, 1992

Rhoda, Rena, Ricky, Rooster, Rowdy and Margaret Rose return home starving, hoping that Mama Rabbit will have dinner waiting. All they find, however, is a note saying Grandma Rabbit is sick with the flu and Mama has gone to care for her. Mama's note tells them to work together to cook something for dinner. Rhonda, too hungry to help, finally realizes that the soup isn't quite ready until she decides to pitch in to help with the cooking. *(ps)*

Group Soup

Have the children work together to make a soup their mothers would be proud of. And then, why not invite the moms to lunch to enjoy this book and a cup of hot homemade group soup?

- 1–2 potatoes
- 2–3 carrots
- ½ lb. fresh green beans
- 2–3 small turnips
- 2 stalks celery
- handful fresh parsley
- 2–3 bouillon cubes
- water or chicken stock

Have children chop vegetables and put into a large soup pot. Add water to cover plus two additional cups. Bring to a boil. Add bouillon and seasonings to taste. Let simmer about ½ hour.

To Market, To Market

Anne Miranda • Illustrated by Janet Stevens
Harcourt Brace, 1997

"To market, to market to buy a fat pig … ." Thus begins this story about a shopper who buys a goose, a trout, a hen, a lamb and other live animals at the market. When she takes them home, they wreak havoc in her kitchen. She returns to market one last time for rice, spices and vegetables and prepares hot soup to serve to her newly acquired friends. *(ps, pm)*

Soup

- 1 onion, chopped
- 2 stalks celery, chopped
- 1 beet, cubed
- 2 tomatoes, cubed
- ½ lb. fresh pea pods
- 1 green pepper, chopped, seeds removed
- 1 clove garlic, minced
- 1 small head of cabbage, shredded
- 2 okra, chopped
- 3 carrots, sliced
- ½ cup brown rice
- 6–7 cups water

Have children chop, cube and dice the vegetables. Put into large soup pot. Add water. Stir in brown rice. Bring to a boil. Turn down the heat and simmer about an hour, until vegetables are tender and rice is done.

My Kitchen

Harlow Rockwell
Greenwillow, 1980

A child takes the reader on a tour through his kitchen, explaining how he makes his lunch of chicken noodle soup, a peanut butter sandwich, and milk. *(ps)*

Soup and Sandwich

- 2 large cans chicken noodle soup
- bread
- peanut butter
- milk

Each child makes his or her own sandwich and pours a glass of milk. Serve with a bowl of soup.

Kevin's Grandma

Barbara Williams • Illustrated by Kay Choaro
E. P. Dutton, 1975

Kevin's grandma is like no other. She scuba dives, jumps from airplanes, climbs mountains, and makes homemade peanut butter soup! "Whoever heard of peanut butter soup?"

Actually, peanut butter soup is very popular in Africa. After your students make this soup, perhaps they will believe the other exciting things about Kevin's grandma. *(all ages)*

Peanut Butter Soup

- 4 cans (14½ oz.) chicken broth
- 16-oz. jar peanut butter
- 1 medium onion, chopped
- 1 tablespoon cornstarch
- 1½ cups half-and-half
- salt and pepper
- sprig of fresh parsley

Heat the chicken broth, peanut butter, and onion. Bring to a boil, stirring occasionally. Mix cornstarch with the half-and-half. Add this mixture to the soup. Add salt and pepper to taste. Simmer for 30 minutes. Garnish with fresh parsley.

Chop, Simmer, Season

Alexa Brandenberg
Harcourt Brace, 1997

This book uses very simple text, one word per page as the characters "chop, simmer and season" in their kitchen. *(ps)*

Minestrone

- 2 –3 lbs. beef soup bones
- 3 quarts water
- 1 bay leaf
- 2 cloves garlic, minced
- 2 teaspoons salt
- ¼ teaspoon pepper
- 1 onion, chopped
- ¼ cup parsley
- 2 cups cabbage, chopped
- 5 carrots, sliced
- 2 stalks celery, sliced
- 1 can tomatoes
- 1 can tomato sauce
- 2 cups fresh spinach, chopped
- Parmesan cheese

In a large pot, add water, bay leaf, garlic, salt and pepper and soup bones. Bring to a boil. Reduce heat, cover pot and simmer for 3 hours. Remove meat from bones. Discard bones. Add remaining ingredients except spinach. Simmer for an hour, adding spinach the last 15 minutes. Sprinkle with Parmesan cheese and serve hot.

More recipes for this book on pages 76 and 92.

"Birthday Soup" from Little Bear

Else Holmelund • Illustrated by Maurice Sendak
Harper and Row, 1957

When Little Bear thinks his mother has forgotten to bake a cake for his birthday, he makes birthday soup for his friends who come to celebrate with him. While they are eating, Mother arrives with a surprise—a big birthday cake. She didn't forget his birthday after all! *(ps, pm)*

Birthday Soup

Instead of assigning a specific vegetable to each child in class, ask them to bring in any vegetable to put into the soup. You might want to add cans of beef or chicken broth and some meat to the soup. Let children wash and cut up the vegetables they've chosen. Add enough water to cover the vegetables and cook until tender. What a wonderful birthday surprise soup!

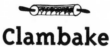

Clambake

Russell M. Peters • Photographs by John Madama
Lerner, 1992

Steven Peters is a Wampanoag Indian living in modern day Plymouth, Massachusetts. In this nonfiction book, Steven's grandfather shares the culture and traditions of the Wampanoag Indians with him, including the appanaug, or clambake. The book details a traditional clambake which you could recreate, or you can taste quahog clams in this chowder. *(pm, in)*

Quahog Chowder

- ½ pound salt pork
- 4 onions
- 5-6 potatoes
- salt and pepper to taste
- 1 quart quahogs, in liquor
- 2 tablespoons tomato soup

Cook salt pork until crisp. Drain on paper towels. Chop onions and add to fat from pork, saute. Chop potatoes and add to onions. Salt and pepper to taste. Drain liquor from quahogs, reserve. Measure how much liquor there is and put in pot. Pour in water to equal the amount of liquor. Bring to a boil, turn down the heat and simmer 20 minutes. Chop quahogs and add to the pot. Heat a while longer. Add tomato soup. Serve hot.

Food Fight

Edited and illustrated by Michael J. Rosen
Harcourt Brace, 1996

Michael Rosen has chosen food-related poems by such poets as Jack Prelutsky, J. Patrick Lewis and Crescent Dragonwagon. Included here is a recipe to be made after reading "Matzo Ball Soup." *(all ages)*

Matzo Ball Soup

- 2 beef bones
- 2 quarts of water
- chicken pieces
- 2 chicken bullion cubes
- 3 carrots
- 2 onions
- 2 stalks celery

Simmer beef bones, covered for 1 hour. Add chicken and bullion cubes. Add vegetables and salt and pepper to taste. Cover and simmer another hour.

Matzo Balls

- 3 eggs, beaten until frothy
- ¾ cup matzo meal

Beat eggs in a bowl. Add matzo meal, and salt and pepper to taste. Mix well. Let stand for 15 minutes. Wet hands, sprinkle some matzo meal in hands and roll mixture to make small balls. Heat soup to a boil, add matzo balls, cover pan and cook over medium heat for 20 minutes.

More recipes for this book on page 39.

Famous Seaweed Soup

Antoinette Truglio Martin • Illustrated by Nadine Bernard Westcott
Albert Whitman, 1993

When Sara and her family go to the beach, Sara wants help making her famous seaweed soup. Since everyone in her family is too busy to help, she makes her soup all by herself. She adds water, feathers, beach glass and other beach treasures to her pretend soup. Young children will immediately notice the familiar pattern from *The Little Red Hen.* *(ps, pm)*

"Seaweed Soup"

Though Sara's seaweed soup is just pretend, in Korea and other Asian countries they really do eat a soup made from kelp, or seaweed. Even though they do not eat this soup in the book, a recipe is included so you can introduce your children to a taste from another culture. You may want to make jelly sandwiches with your children as well.

- 4 ounces dried wakame*
- 6 cups fish, chicken or beef stock
- 1 bunch green onions
- 1 tablespoon sesame oil
- 2 cloves garlic, minced
- ¼ – ½ lb beef or chicken
- sesame seeds

Soak wakame in water for 30 minutes. Drain and cut into strips. Pour soup stock into pan, bring to a boil. After soup stock boils, turn heat to low and simmer. Saute garlic and meat in sesame oil in a skillet. Add meat, and wakame to soup stock. Simmer for 15 more minutes.

*A type of seaweed available from health food stores or Asian grocery stores.

More recipes for this book on page 35.

My Side of the Mountain

Jean George

Dutton, 1959 ★ Newbery Honor Book

Sam Gribley sets out to live completely alone in a remote area of the Catskill Mountains. He builds a shelter in a tree and lives off the land for all his needs. Sam eats various types of food that he gathers or hunts in the woods, including deer, mussels, rabbit, acorns, tubers of wild flowers, and sassafras root. Your children might want to enjoy rabbit stew while reading this book. *(in)*

Rabbit Stew

- 2½ lbs. rabbit, pieced
- 1¼ cups water
- ¾ cup vinegar
- 1 onion
- 2 bay leaves
- 8 whole cloves
- 2 teaspoons salt
- ½ teaspoon pepper
- ⅓ cup flour
- ⅓ cup shortening
- 2 tablespoons brown sugar
- 1 cup sour cream

Put rabbit in a glass bowl and cover with water and vinegar. Add onion and spices, reserving 1 teaspoon of salt for later, and cover. Marinate in refrigerator for three days. Remove the meat from marinade but do not discard marinade; coat meat with flour and remaining salt. Fry in hot shortening, turning frequently, until brown. Strain 1 cup vinegar and water mixture to remove pieces of spices. Add brown sugar to strained marinade and pour over meat. Cover and simmer until tender. Add sour cream just before serving; do not boil.

The Talking Eggs

Robert D. Sans Souci • Illustrated by Jerry Pinkney

Scholastic, 1989 ★ Caldecott Honor Book

Blanche and Rose are sisters who live on a very poor farm with their mother. Blanche is the younger sister and she is very kind and sweet. Rose, the older, is cross and mean and Mother's favorite. On separate occasions, each sister meets a strange woman in the woods and is invited to her home. There the girls see unusual animals and many strange events. Each of the girls reacts to the woman and her unusual cabin with different and deserving results. Because of her kindness and the woman's powers, Blanche is able to make stew with just a few pieces of rice. This stew will take more than rice to prepare, but is perfect to enjoy after reading this traditional Cajun folktale. *(pm, in)*

Stew

- 1 – 1½ lbs. stew meat
- flour
- cooking oil
- ½ cup water
- 4–5 carrots, sliced
- 1 can tomato soup
- 10 fresh mushrooms
- 1 stalk celery
- 4–5 potatoes, cut into chunks
- salt and pepper to taste

Roll stew meat in flour. In a skillet, brown beef in 2 tablespoons cooking oil. Place browned beef in a baking pan. Add remaining ingredients. Cover and bake for 1½ hours at 325°. Add water if needed. Cover and bake an additional 45 minutes.

More recipes for this book on page 59.

The Big Stew!

Ben Shecter
HarperCollins, 1991

A man and his wife decide to make stew adding "a little of this; a little of that." Illustrations show the couple busy adding ingredients such as tomatoes and eggplant to make their stew, but everything changes as the pair begins adding snakes, eye balls and other gross items. The characters are transformed into witches as the ingredient list changes. Finally, the couple realizes what should really go into their stew, and the stew ends up being "Perfect!" The couple changes back into the original husband and wife who enjoy a hearty stew together. Easy for children to read on their own. *(ps, pm)*

With the children, decide what ingredients should go into a perfect stew and using the recipe below as a base, make stew. Include the items the children decide on. You may also want to make flannelboard pieces of the ingredients from the book so the children can retell this story during the Halloween season.

Stew

- 2 lbs. stewing beef chunks
- 2 tablespoons flour
- 1 teaspoon salt
- pepper, to taste
- 2 tablespoons vegetable oil
- 2 cups water
- 1 large onion
- 5–7 carrots
- 4–5 potatoes
- canned or fresh tomatoes

Combine flour, salt and pepper. Cut the beef into 1-inch pieces. Cover the meat with flour mixture. Brown meat and onions in oil in a large pot. Add water, bring to a boil. Simmer for 1½ to 2 hours, adding water as necessary. Add onions, carrots and potatoes. Simmer 30 minutes longer, adding tomatoes the last 15 minutes. If you desire a thicker stew, mix 1to 2 tablespoons flour to cold water and add to stew the last half hour.

Merry Christmas, Strega Nona

Tomie dePaola
Harcourt Brace Jovanovich, 1986

Here's another adventure with Big Anthony and Strega Nona. This time Strega Nona almost doesn't have her annual Christmas celebration because of Big Anthony's laziness. He forgets to soak the codfish—the baccala—for the codfish stew. What will Strega Nona do? *(all ages)*

Codfish Stew

- ½ lb. codfish in bite-sized pieces
- 2–3 potatoes
- 1–2 stalks of celery
- 1–2 onions
- 2–3 garlic cloves
- ½ teaspoon thyme
- 1½ teaspoons dried parsley
- corn, peas, green pepper, mushrooms, or other vegetables

Baccala, or dried salt cod, needs to be soaked for several days before using. If you cannot find dried salt cod, substitute fresh or frozen cod. But if the children can see how long it takes to prepare the salt cod before it can be cooked, they will better understand why Strega Nona is so disappointed with Big Anthony.

Wash the salted cod under cold running water, then totally immerse in cold water, cover, and keep in the refrigerator 24 to 48 hours. Change the water two or three times during this soaking period. When ready to cook, place the cod in boiling water and simmer 15 minutes. Drain. When cool, remove bones and skin. Chop the vegetables and simmer all ingredients about 15 minutes.

Pueblo Storyteller

Diane Hoyt-Goldsmith • Photographs by Lawrence Migdale
Holiday House, 1991

This nonfiction story introduces the reader to April, a young Native American girl, who lives on the Cochiti Pueblo near Santa Fe, New Mexico. The book describes her family, culture and customs, showing how the family bakes bread and makes clay storytellers. Making posole will give children a taste of the food that April and her family enjoy. *(pm, in)*

Posole

- 1 lb. cubed pork
- 1 tablespoon olive oil
- 2 cups posole*

- 2 teaspoons chili powder
- 6 cups water

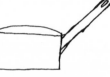

Brown pork in olive oil. Combine cooked pork and other ingredients in a sauce pan. Cook until posole gets soft and open. Add salt to taste.

* available from Mexican markets or health food stores

Pigs in the Pantry

Amy Axelrod • Illustrated Sharon McGinley-Nally
Simon & Schuster, 1997

When Mrs. Pig feels under the weather, Mr. Pig and their two children decide to make her favorite dish. As one might predict, Mrs. Pig gets little rest while her family creates a mess in the kitchen, including a visit from the fire department. The book includes Mrs. Pig's favorite meal, Firehouse Chili, or you can make the mild chili below. Just be sure to clean up the kitchen! *(ps, pm)*

Chili

- 1 lb. ground beef
- 1 onion, chopped
- 2 stalks celery, chopped
- ½ green pepper, chopped

- 1 can chili beans
- 1 can kidney beans, drained
- 1 can tomato soup, plus can of water

Brown ground beef in a skillet. Add onion, celery and green pepper. When vegetables are tender, add soup and water and both cans of beans. Add ½ chili can more water. Heat to a boil, then simmer for 45 minutes to an hour.

Pizza

The Rattlebang Picnic

Margaret Mahy • Illustrated by Steven Kellogg
Dial, 1994

Much to the delight of Granny McTarish, her son and his wife have decided to have seven children and drive an old rattlebang car, rather than have a fancy car and no children. When the family all goes on a picnic, they are disappointed with Granny's tough, hard pizza, and they settle on a picnic with cupcakes and apples. But when the old rattlebang car breaks down, it is Granny's pizza that saves the day! *(all ages)*

Pizza

If you don't cook it as long as Granny does, it should stay soft and edible.

- 1 can refrigerator biscuits
- spaghetti or pizza sauce
- mozzarella cheese
- pepperoni, cooked hamburger or veggies

Give each child a piece of aluminum foil and a biscuit. Have them flatten biscuits with their hands or a rolling pin. Place on an ungreased cookie sheet. Spread sauce on top, cover with cheese and choice of toppings. Bake at 350° for 15 to 20 minutes or until cheese has melted.

Pizza for Breakfast

Maryann Kovalski
Morrow Junior Books, 1990

Frank and his wife Zelda own a pizza shop next to Mel's Summer Hat and Glove Factory. Each day the factory workers come for lunch and in the evening, shop owners come for dinner. Business at Frank and Zelda's is booming! As time goes on people stop wearing hats and gloves in the summer and the factory closes. Frank and Zelda's pizza shop suffers as the workers no longer come to eat. One day a stranger stops by to eat, but is unable to pay. In return for his meal he tells Frank and Zelda that he will grant them anything that they wish for. At first they are pleased with their good fortune, but things soon get out of hand. Be careful what you wish for! *(ps, pm)*

Pizza

- 2 cups biscuit mix
- ⅔ cup milk
- can tomato sauce
- cheese
- pepperoni or cooked ground hamburger
- salt, pepper, garlic salt, to taste
- olive oil

Combine biscuit mix and milk. Knead on a floured surface until smooth. Divide into four equal portions of dough. Roll out to about 5 to 6 inches in diameter. Add sauce, cheese and toppings of your choice. Bake at 425° for 15 to 20 minutes until cheese melts.

Curious George and the Pizza
Margaret and H. A. Rey
Scholastic, 1985

As usual, George's curiosity gets him into some comical troubles. This time George finds himself in a pizza parlor. Sometimes local pizza parlors will allow you to take your class in to make their own individual pizzas. Or you might choose to make pizza at school. If you want your children to experience kneading their own crust, see the recipe under *Little Nino's Pizzeria* below. *(ps, pm)*

Pizza

- 2 frozen pizza crusts
- 2 cans pizza or tomato sauce
- cooked hamburger, pepperoni, or sausage
- onions, green peppers, mushrooms, if desired
- 1½–2 lbs. mozzarella cheese

Students can take turns grating the cheese. Place the crusts onto two pizza pans, and add tomato sauce and desired toppings. Bake at 400° for 8 to 9 minutes or until the cheese starts to brown.

Little Nino's Pizzeria
Karen Barbour
Harcourt Brace Jovanovich, 1987 ★ Reading Rainbow Selection

When Nino, the pizza maker, closes his family-run pizzeria, "Little Nino's," and opens up a big, fancy, expensive restaurant called "Big Nino's," he finds the paperwork and the money talk has taken over what he really wants to do—make pizza! This book can be enjoyed as a story, as well as an introduction to comparing small businesses and large businesses. *(all ages)*

Pizza

- 1 pkg. hot roll mix
- 1½ cups hot water
- 2 tablespoons cooking oil
- cornmeal
- 8-oz. can pizza sauce
- oregano
- mozzarella cheese
- cooked hamburger or pepperoni
- onions, finely chopped
- green pepper, diced

Combine hot roll mix, hot water, and oil. Mix well. Let the children take turns kneading the dough for about 5 minutes. Give each child a piece of dough about the size of a golf ball and a small square of greased aluminum foil. Have the children sprinkle a small amount of cornmeal onto the foil and flatten their dough into a circle, forming their pizza crust. Allow the children to spoon a small amount of pizza sauce and other toppings onto their mini pizzas. Place the foil squares onto cookie sheets. You can write their names on the foil with a permanent marker. Bake at 425° for 12 to 15 minutes.

Pizza!

Teresa Martino • Illustrated by Brigid Faranda
Steck-Vaughn, 1992

The history of pizza is told from its simple beginnings as a flat piece of dough made by a woman wanting something to eat while she baked bread over 1,000 years ago to the pizza we have today. One hundred years ago a pizza baker named Raffaele Esposito made pizza much like children eat today, but it had no cheese on it. Mr. Esposito put fresh tomatoes and basil leaves on his pizza, and people thought it was the best in Italy. When the king of Italy asked Esposito to make a pizza for Queen Margherita, he wanted to create a new kind of pizza especially for her. He decided to use the colors of the Italian flag, red, white and green—red tomatoes, green basil leaves and white cheese. Today you can order pizza in Italy—Pizza Margherita—named after this queen. *(pm, in)*

Pizza

Use pizza dough of your choice—handmade, frozen or pita bread. If you use pita bread, each child can make their own pizza. Have the children cut fresh tomatoes and mozzarella cheese into thin slices. Top the dough or pita bread with tomatoes, cheese and fresh basil leaves. Bake 10 to 20 minutes, depending on size of pizzas, at 350° until cheese melts.

The King of Pizza

Sylvester Sanzari • Illustrated by John E. Hurst
Workman, 1995

There was once a king who ate more food than any other man in his kingdom. He even made a special decree to have his dinner served two hours early so he would have time for several desserts. But no matter how much he ate, he was never satisfied. One morning after thinking of food all night long, he sneaked into town and learned about generosity and sharing from Salvatore, the owner and cook of the town's pizzeria. The king learned Salvatore's secret recipe for pizza— "… the most important ingredient in any meal … is the love that you add when you share it." The king celebrates with a party, shares his food with others and never loses sleep on account of his hunger again. *(all ages)*

Pizza

You may use any of the recipes for pizza included in *Cook-A-Book*, or use the recipes for pizza dough and toppings presented at the end of *The King of Pizza*.

Pizza Man

Marjorie Pillar
Cromwell, 1990

This is the perfect nonfiction book to share with your class before you go on a field trip to the pizzeria. You see how pizza is made behind the scenes at a restaurant. Black and white photographs show the big mixer, oven and other equipment. *(all ages)*

Pizza

Use one of the recipes in this section to make a pizza at school. But to get the full effect of this book a trip to a local pizzeria is in order. Try to schedule a trip to a pizza parlor that will allow each child or a pair of children to create their own pizzas.

Extra Cheese, Please

Cris Peterson • Photographs by Alvis Upitis
Boyd Mills, 1994

This nonfiction book explains how cheese is made at a dairy farm. Colorful photographs show how the cheese starts as milk from the cows with clear text that explain how the milk is made into cheese. The book concludes with children making a pizza using the newly made cheese. This book would work well with a trip to the farm or pizzeria. *(all ages)*

Pizza

Use one of the recipes for pizza found in this section.

Hold the Anchovies

Shelley Rotner and Julia Pemberton Hellums • Photographs by Shelley Rotner
Orchard Books, 1996

A beautifully illustrated photo essay explains not only how pizza is made, but also how grain and tomatoes are grown and how cheese is made—all important ingredients in making pizza. The book includes very clever endpapers. A recipe for making pizza is included in the book. *(all ages)*

Chocolate Chip Cookie Contest

Barbara Douglass
Lothrop, Lee & Shepard, 1985

Kevin plans to enter the chocolate chip cookie contest at the mall, but he needs to find an adult to help him use the oven. Every adult he asks is too busy to help, but each gives some advice as to what ingredient is missing from his recipe. When he finally finds a grown-up to help him, they make a chocolate chip pizza. Do they win the contest? You be the judge when you make the chocolate chip pizza using the recipe included in the book. *(pm, in)*

Chocolate Chip Pizza

Have each child bring six of his or her favorite chocolate chip cookies to school. Make the chocolate chip pizza using the recipe in the book and have your own Chocolate Chip Contest. Taste all the different types of cookies. Have a blue ribbon for each child to award to the cookie he or she likes the best. Be sure each child receives a ribbon by creating a variety of categories: biggest, smallest, most chips, etc. This way each will have a ribbon to take home to remember the day's activities.

 # Pasta, Rice

Spaghetti and Meatballs for All!
Marilyn Burns • Illustrated by Debbie Tilley
Scholastic, 1997

Mr. and Mrs. Comfort plan a family reunion and invite 32 people, including themselves. Making the meal, spaghetti and meatballs, for everyone is simple enough. But things begin to get more complicated when they try to arrange the table and chairs.

Part of Marilyn Burns' Brainy Day Math Book series, this book inspires readers to use their math skills to help the Comforts solve their seating problems. *(pm, in)*

Spaghetti Dinner

After reading this story, plan a spaghetti dinner with your class. You can use packaged pasta, but the best way to prepare the meal, if you have the time, is to make fresh pasta. See the recipe for homemade pasta that goes with *Strega Nona* on page 58. Since a pasta machine is used in *Spaghetti and Meatballs for All*, you may want to use a pasta machine to roll out the dough, rather than having the children roll it with a rolling pin.

If having the whole class make all four parts of the meal is too difficult, divide the children into four groups. Choose one group to make the garlic bread; another to make the tomato, lettuce and cucumber salad; and the last two groups to make the pasta and meatballs and sauce.

Garlic Bread

Have each child butter a slice of fresh bread. Sprinkle with garlic powder and bake or grill in a frying pan until butter is melted and the bread is crisp and brown.

Fresh Pasta

See the recipe on page 58 for making homemade pasta.

Salad

- 3–4 tomatoes
- 1 cucumber
- head of lettuce

While some children in class are setting the table or making other parts of the meal, ask a small group to wash and cut the tomatoes, cucumbers and lettuce for the salad.

Meatballs and Sauce

- 2 lbs. ground beef
- 1 package dry onion soup mix
- 1 cup bread crumbs
- 2 eggs
- ½ teaspoon pepper
- 3-4 large jars of spaghetti sauce

Mix ingredients together in bowl. Form into meatballs and fry in a skillet. Add jars of prepared spaghetti sauce and simmer for ½ hour.

Siggy's Spaghetti Works

Peggy Thomson • Illustrated by Gloria Kamen
Tambourine Books, 1993

Siggy owns a spaghetti factory and loves to make pasta. The children in the book are given a tour of Siggy's factory and learn how pasta dough is mixed, formed and packaged. Also included is historical information about pasta around the world. Reading this book will put you in the mood to make and eat several types of pasta. Try making pasta from scratch and use a pasta machine to cut your noodles into a variety of forms, or purchase different pasta shapes to share with your class. *(pm, in)*

Pasta from Scratch with Pasta Machine and Variety of Pastas

See the recipe below for homemade pasta. Instead of rolling the dough by hand you may want to use a pasta machine and cut a variety of pasta shapes. If you don't want to make pasta from scratch you can buy several varieties and shapes of pasta from the grocery store or a gourmet food shop. Look for rigatoni, tortellini, penne, angel hair, vermicelli, mostacolli and others. Cook pasta until it is *al denté*, which means "to the tooth." *Al denté* pasta is not cooked until mushy. Serve with butter and cheese or your favorite sauce.

Curious George Takes a Job

H. A. Rey
Scholastic, 1947

Curious George really wants to know what is going on outside the zoo. He escapes and soon discovers a restaurant kitchen with a pot of spaghetti cooking on the stove. When you cook this spaghetti, watch out for curious monkeys! *(ps, pm)*

Spaghetti

Follow the directions on the box to prepare 1 lb. of spaghetti. In the book, George eats the noodles right from the pot, with no sauce. Your students might want to try it this way, or with butter and a sprinkle of garlic powder and Parmesan cheese.

Strega Nona

Tomie dePaola
Prentice Hall, 1975 ★ Caldecott Honor Book

Strega Nona owns a magic pasta pot and warns her helper, Big Anthony, never to touch it. One day when Strega Nona goes out, Big Anthony makes pasta with the magic pot. When Strega Nona returns, she knows what has happened because there is pasta covering the town. How does all this get cleaned up in time for Strega Nona to sleep in her bed that night? *(all ages)*

Homemade Pasta

- 1½ cups flour
- ½ teaspoon salt
- 2 eggs, beaten
- 1 stick margarine
- 4-oz. can Parmesan cheese

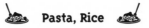

Combine flour, salt, and eggs. On a lightly floured cutting board, let the children roll out the dough until it is thin. Allow each child to cut noodles into strips with a knife. Let the children break the noodles until they are approximately 3 inches long. Place noodles into boiling water and cook until tender. Drain. Mix in the margarine and can of cheese.

Have an adult with each group of 8 to 10 children making the recipe above. A pasta machine can be used, but the children learn more if they have to roll the dough themselves. Cook all pasta together in a large pot.

Spaghetti Eddie
Mary Ellis
T. S. Denison, 1957

Eddie and his sister, Joan, make a spaghetti for dinner to surprise their mother when she comes home from work. Eddie insists that more spaghetti is needed and convinces a delivery man to add more to the pot when he comes to deliver groceries. When they end up with more spaghetti than they can eat, Eddie delivers bowls of pasta to neighbors and friends. Make enough spaghetti so your students can deliver some to the teachers, secretary, principal, and other friends at school. *(ps, pm)*

Spaghetti

- 1 lb. hamburger
- 1 pkg. spaghetti seasonings
- 1 pkg. spaghetti noodles
- 6-oz. can tomato paste
- 1¾ cups water

Brown the hamburger in a skillet. Drain off grease. Add the seasonings, tomato paste, and water. Simmer about 30 minutes. Prepare spaghetti noodles. Serve hot with Parmesan cheese.

This Is the Way We Eat Our Lunch
Edith Bauer • Illustrated by Steve Bjorkman
See main entry on page 1

Cous Cous

An easy cous cous can be made by purchasing a box of cous cous, found in health food stores or specialty food sections of the grocery store. Follow directions on the package. *(ps, pm)*

The Talking Eggs
Robert D. Sans Souci • Illustrated by Jerry Pinkney
See main entry on page 50

Rice

Make your favorite rice—white rice, balsamic rice, brown rice or wild rice and cook according to the directions on the package. Serve with the stew on page 50. *(pm, in)*

The Sacred Harvest
Ojibwa Wild Rice Gathering
Gordon Regguinti • Photographs by Dale Kakkak
Lerner, 1992

This nonfiction book follows Glen Jackson, Jr., an 11-year-old Ojibwa Indian living in Minnesota, as he harvests wild rice with his father. The wild rice is a sacred food of the Ojibwa people. *(pm,in)*

Wild Rice

If possible, buy wild rice from the Leech Lake Reservation that is spotlighted in *The Sacred Harvest*. If you are unable to find wild rice from this reservation, buy the wild rice that is available locally. Prepare according to directions on the package.

Hoang Anh
A Vietnamese American Boy
Diane Hoyt-Goldsmith • Photographs by Lawrence Migdale
See main entry on page 37

Rice

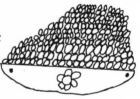

Prepare rice according to directions on the package, usually 1 cup of rice to 2 cups of water. Cover and heat until water boils, lower heat and cook covered for 20 minutes. Serve hot cooked rice with chopsticks.

How My Parents Learned to Eat
Ina R. Friedman • Illustrated by Allen Say
Houghton Mifflin, 1984 ★ Reading Rainbow Selection

When an American sailor and a Japanese woman marry, their daughter learns to eat both with a fork and with chopsticks. You can prepare rice with your students and teach them how to use chopsticks. Wooden chopsticks can be purchased very inexpensively. Let each child have a pair to use and take home. *(all ages)*

White Rice

- 1 cup white rice
- 2 cups water
- 1 tablespoon oil or butter

Combine the rice, water, and butter in a 1-quart sauce pan. Bring to a boil. Cover pan with lid. Turn heat down to low and simmer for 20 minutes.

Fish, Meat

Aunt Flossie's Hat (and Crab Cakes Later)

Elizabeth Fitzgerald Howard • Illustrated by James Ransome
Clarion, 1991

On Sundays, Susan and Sarah visit with their Great-Great Aunt Flossie. They love her house crowded with books, lamps, pictures, pillows, and boxes and boxes and boxes of hats. As the girls try on Aunt Flossie's hats, she shares stories and memories that each hat represents. Later they all have crab cakes—which taste much better after stories about Aunt Flossie's hats. *(all ages)*

Crab Cakes

- 1 lb. crab meat
- ½ teaspoon seafood seasoning
- pepper or hot sauce to taste
- 1½ teaspoons Worcestershire
- ½ cup bread crumbs
- 1 egg, beaten
- flour
- vegetable oil

Combine all ingredients, except flour and oil. Make 8 to 10 patties. Flour each pattie and fry in oil until brown.

More recipes for this book on page 86.

Fish for Supper

M. B. Goffstein
E. P. Dutton, 1976 ★ Caldecott Honor Book

Grandmother loves to get up at five o'clock in the morning and go fishing all day. She comes home in the evening and fries her catch for supper. She cleans up fast, so she can go to bed and get up and go fishing again.

If you can take your class fishing, you can prepare your catch at school the next day. If not, buy some fresh or frozen fish at the store. *(ps, pm)*

Fried Fish

- 1 egg yolk
- ½ cup ice water
- ¾ cup self-rising flour
- 1–2 lbs. cod fillets or other fish, at least ½" thick

In a mixing bowl, beat the egg yolk; add ice water and beat again until well blended. Add flour and stir in, but do not stir until smooth; mixture should be lumpy. The batter must be kept cold. You might want to make the batter and store it in the refrigerator for a couple of hours before cooking. Heat cooking oil in an electric skillet. When the oil is hot, dip the fish into the batter and fry until crispy and golden brown.

Fishing at Long Pond

William T. George • Illustrated by Lindsay Barrett George
Greenwillow, 1991

Katie and her grandfather row to the edge of the pond to catch bass for dinner. Grandfather shares the day and the natural world with Katie in this beautifully illustrated book. *(all ages)*

Bass

- 1½ lbs. bass
- 3 tablespoons cornmeal
- 3 tablespoons flour
- dash of salt and pepper
- olive oil

Combine dry ingredients. Coat fish with flour and cornmeal mixture. Pan fry fish in 1 tablespoon olive oil until brown. Turn and brown second side. Cook this over an outdoor fire if possible. I am sure Katie and her grandfather did!

Fishy, Fishy in the Brook

Traditional Mother Goose

Fishy, fishy in the brook,
Daddy caught him on a hook,
Mommy fried him in a pan,
Baby eats him like a man.

Fish Sticks

Fry up 1 or 2 fish sticks per child in a small amount of oil in an electric skillet. If you want to fry fresh or frozen fish, see the recipe listed under *Fish for Supper* on page 61. *(ps, pm)*

The Great Brain

John D. Fitzgerald
Dell, 1975

Tom Fitzgerald, better known as The Great Brain, is always scheming for ways to get out of household chores and to make money. Tom loves eating all kinds of fish because fish is known as brain food. You might enjoy tasting codfish, as Tom does in this book. *(pm, in)*

Codfish

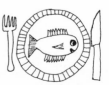

- 2–4 lbs. cod fillets
- salt and pepper
- cornmeal
- butter and lemon

Sprinkle the salt, pepper, and cornmeal on fish. Melt 2 tablespoons of butter in a pan. Brown fish in butter; turn and brown other side. Serve with melted butter and lemon wedges.

Mrs. Katz and Tush

Patricia Polacco
Bantam Little Rooster Book, 1992

Larnel, an African American boy, befriends Mrs. Katz, an elderly Jewish woman. Mrs. Katz shares stories from her life with Larnel and he learns that Jews, like African Americans, were enslaved and forced to live where they did not want to. Mrs. Katz talks about Passover and the seder with him. Years later, when Larnel has grown and has his first child, Mrs. Katz is still a part of his family. *(pm, in)*

Gefilte Fish

Gefilte fish is a popular dish eaten during Jewish holidays. As Jewish cooking has become more "Americanized," many traditional dishes have developed regional variations based on the availability of ingredients. In this way, a variety of fish are used for gefilte fish—whitefish is often used in the Midwest, salmon in the West and haddock in Maine.

- 3 lbs. white fresh fish
- ¼ cup matzo meal
- 1 cup cold water
- 1 egg
- 2 onions, peeled
- 1 stalk celery
- salt and pepper

Remove bone and skin from fish, removing whole skin. Save both skin and bones. Wash skin with water. In a separate bowl add matzo meal, salt and pepper, water and egg. Mix well. Place matzo meal mixture inside skin of fish. In a pot, boil fish bones, onion and celery until tender. Add fish to pot. Simmer until well done, about a hour. Add water to pot if necessary. Serve hot.

More recipes for this book on page 12.

King Bob's New Clothes

Dom DeLuise • Illustrated by Christopher Santoro
Simon & Schuster, 1996

When Dom DeLuise adds his wit and humor to the traditional tale, "The Emperor's New Clothes," you can be sure of a few chuckles and some merriment. When the king arrives in town to show off his new wardrobe, many of the townsfolk bring picnic lunches of king crab cakes, chicken à la king and kings in a blanket. These recipes and one for king crown cake are included at the end of the book—or you may wish to use the recipe for chicken à la king below. *(all ages)*

Chicken à la King

- ¼ cup butter or margarine
- 3 tablespoons flour
- 1 cup chicken broth
- 1 cup milk
- 2 cups chicken
- ½ teaspoon salt
- onion salt, seasoned salt, pepper, parsley
- egg noodles or toast

Melt butter. Blend in flour. Add chicken broth and milk slowly to flour mixture. Add chicken, salt and other seasonings to taste. Serve hot over toast or egg noodles.

Three Days on a River in a Red Canoe

Vera B. Williams

Greenwillow, 1981 ★ A Reading Rainbow Book

If you are fortunate enough to take your class on a camping trip, making these recipes outside will make cooking more authentic. If a camping trip isn't possible, maybe you could make this at a national, state or city park. If you want to make it indoors, I would suggest setting up a tent and "camp ground" on your school grounds. *(all ages)*

Chicken and Rice

- 1 cup rice
- 2 stalks celery, chopped
- 4–5 green onions, chopped
- 2 cans cream of chicken soup
- 1 small can chicken broth
- 1 can mushrooms
- 2 chickens, cut-up pieces
- ½ stick butter or margarine, melted

In a baking pan, sprinkle rice evenly on the bottom. Add celery and green onions. In a separate bowl, mix chicken soup, chicken broth and mushrooms together. Pour over rice. Roll chicken pieces in melted butter or margarine and place on rice. Season with salt and pepper if desired. Bake in a greased casserole dish at 325° for 2 hours.

More recipes for this book on page 74.

The Magic Meatballs

Alan Yaffe • Illustrated by Karen Born Andersen

Dial, 1979

Poor Marvin—everyone bosses him around, until he eats the magic meatballs, that is. Then unusual things begin to happen at home. Be careful who you share your magic meatballs with! *(ps, pm)*

Magic Meatballs

- 1 egg, slightly beaten
- ½ cup milk
- 2 slices bread, diced
- 1 lb. hamburger
- ¼ teaspoon pepper
- 1 onion, finely chopped
- ½ teaspoon salt
- 2–3 teaspoons butter

Combine all the ingredients except the butter. Each child makes a 1-inch meatball. Brown the meatballs in butter using an electric skillet.

On Top of Spaghetti

Tom Glazer • Illustrated by Tom Garcia

Doubleday, 1963

This book is an illustrated version of the popular silly song "On Top of Spaghetti." Included with the pictures are the music and words to the song. You might even want to plant a meatball to see if you can grow a meatball tree. *(all ages)*

Meatballs

- 1 lb. hamburger
- ½ cup bread crumbs
- 1 egg

- 1 teaspoon salt
- ¼ teaspoon pepper
- 2–3 teaspoons butter

Mix all ingredients except butter in a bowl. Let each child make a small meatball. Brown in an electric skillet, turning meatballs as they cook.

Cloudy with a Chance of Meatballs

Judi Barrett • Illustrated by Ron Barrett
Atheneum, 1978

There are no grocery stores in the town of Chewandswallow. Instead, it rains three times a day—at breakfast, lunch, and dinner. If you would prefer to make a spaghetti-type meatball, see the recipe above. *(all ages)*

Meatballs

- 1 lb. hamburger
- ½ lb. veal
- ¼ lb. pork
- ¾ cup bread crumbs
- 1 egg
- ½ cup chopped onions

- 1 cup milk
- 1½ teaspoons salt
- ½ teaspoon pepper
- ½ teaspoon nutmeg
- dash of allspice and parsley

Mix all ingredients. Let the children shape a meatball or two. Brown meatballs in a skillet. Serve as is, or mix up a package of dry sour cream mix, using about ¼ cup more milk than the directions call for. Coat the meatballs with the sour cream mixture.

The Lost Lake

Allen Say
Houghton Mifflin, 1989

A young Asian boy and his father go on a camping trip to find Lost Lake. Finding it crowded, they continue up the mountain to a secluded area. There, they enjoy the wilderness and solitude as they dine on salami, dried apricots and freeze-dried beef stroganoff. This is the perfect book to share on a camping trip. Talk about why salami, dried apricots and freeze-dried foods are good food to take camping. (These foods are nutritious and easy to carry without a cooler.) What other foods would be good to bring on a backpacking trip? *(all ages)*

Salami and Dried Apricots

Dried apricots are available at most grocery stores. Plan an indoor or outdoor picnic. Or pitch a tent in the classroom, in a park, or near a lake and enjoy slices of salami and dried apricots.

Freeze Dried Beef Stroganoff

Freeze-dried foods are available at camping or outdoor supply stores. Many sports stores also have a camping equipment section where you can buy dried food. Bring this into the class and prepare as directed on the package. Be sure to allow the children to see how this meal is freeze dried and packaged.

Meat Pies and Sausage

Dorothy O. Van Woerhom • Illustrated by Joseph Low
Greenwillow, 1976

In the first of three short stories, a wolf angers a fox by eating his breakfast. When the wolf further torments the fox by threatening to eat him, the fox outwits the wolf. The fox takes the wolf to the house of Ivan and Nessa with the promise of meat pies to eat. They sneak into the cellar. What becomes of the fox and the wolf? *(ps, pm)*

Meat Pies

- 1–1½ lbs. hamburger
- 2 onions, diced
- 1⅓ cups mushrooms
- 1½ teaspoons salt
- 1½ teaspoons pepper
- 1 tube crescent rolls
- 1–1½ cups sour cream
- 2 eggs

Brown hamburger, onions, mushrooms, salt, and pepper. Line a casserole dish with crescent rolls. Pour in hamburger mixture. Blend the sour cream and eggs. Spread over hamburger. Bake at 350° for 35 minutes.

Down Buttermilk Lane

Barbara Mitchell • Illustrated by John Sandford
See main entry on page 100

Green Beans with Ham

- 1 whole cured, ready to eat ham
- whole cloves
- 1 cup maple syrup
- green beans

Trim off any fat and rind from the ham. Score with a knife across top with a diamond pattern. Have the children poke several cloves into the top of the ham. Brush maple syrup evenly over the top. Bake at 325°, uncovered, 10 minutes for every pound. Baste with ¼ cup of syrup every 10 minutes. After using the cup of syrup, baste with ham drippings until done. *(all ages)*

Open several cans of green beans and heat, if you want to make easy beans. If time allows, have the children snap fresh green beans. Steam fresh beans until tender, but not over cooked. Serve hot with the ham.

Don't Forget the Bacon

Pat Hutchins
Greenwillow, 1976

In order to remember the grocery list, a little boy makes a game of the things his mother asks him to buy. He is reminded, "Don't forget the bacon." Guess what he forgets! After reading this book, your children will enjoy eating strips of bacon. *(ps, pm)*

Bacon

Using an electric skillet, have an adult fry up a piece of bacon for each child. Be sure to have plenty of supervision around the hot bacon grease.

An Angel for Solomon Singer

Cynthia Rylant • Illustrated by Peter Catalanottl
See main entry on page 26

Bacon

Since hot grease spatters easily when making bacon have an adult fry the bacon if you are going to serve it with the biscuits from page 26.

Fruits, Vegetables

Turkey Pox

Laurie Halse Anderson • Illustrated by Dorothy Donohue
Albert Whitman, 1996

The Chatfield family is running late for Thanksgiving dinner at Nana's—all except Charity. Charity was ready early because Nana's roast turkey is her favorite food and Thanksgiving is her favorite day. The family finally sets out in a snowstorm for Nana's, only to discover Charity has the chicken pox. Charity fears her favorite day is ruined—until Nana shows up with the turkey, which is dotted with cherry "turkey pox." Try the apple salad below or see page 120 for a full menu. *(ps, pm)*

Apple Salad

- 4–5 apples, chopped
- 1 can crushed pineapple

- 1 cup chopped nuts

Sauce:

- 1 tablespoon flour
- ½ cup cream
- 1 egg

- 2 tablespoons vinegar
- ⅓ cup sugar
- pad of butter

Combine ingredients for sauce in a double boiler. Bring to a boil, stirring constantly. Cool. Pour mixture over fruit.

The Old Woman Who Lived under a Hill

Traditional Mother Goose

There was an old woman
Lived under a hill,
And if she's not gone
She lives there still.

Baked apples she sold
And cranberry pies,
And she's the old woman
Who never told lies.

Baked Apples

- 1 apple per child
- cinnamon

- brown sugar
- whipped cream

Let children wash and core their apples. Put the apples in a cake pan. Have each child fill his or her apple core with brown sugar. Sprinkle with cinnamon. Add enough water to cover the bottom of the pan. Bake for 45 minutes to an hour at 450°. Serve warm with whipped cream.

How Do Apples Grow?

Betsy Maestro • Illustrated by Giulio Maestro
HarperCollins, 1992

This nonfiction look at apples is ideal for the fall season. If possible visit an apple orchard to buy the variety of apples written about in the book. Have an apple tasting party when you return from the trip. If a trip is not possible, the apples listed here should be available in your supermarket. *(all ages)*

Apples

Have an apple tasting party with Granny Smith, Red and Golden Delicious and McIntosh apples. Just slice and eat. Make a graph to find out which type of apple each child likes best.

Rain Makes Applesauce

Julian Scheer • Illustrated by Marvin Bileck
Holiday House, 1964 ★ Caldecott Honor Book

Children love the humor in this book of silly sentences. In addition to the obvious silly sentences and detailed illustrations, please take note of the lower right-hand side of the page, where you will see a little boy and girl planting and caring for an apple tree through the four seasons. In the fall, the apples are picked and the two children make applesauce. *(ps, pm)*

Applesauce

- 1 cooking apple per child
- water
- 2 teaspoons cinnamon

Have the children quarter and core the apples. Be sure to remove all seeds. Put the apple pieces in a large pot. Add ½ to ¾ cup of water and the cinnamon. Add water if needed as the apples cook down. Cook until apples are mushy. If you want a smoother applesauce, peel the apples before cooking or put them through a food mill after cooking.

The Seven Silly Eaters

Mary Ann Hoberman • Illustrated by Marla Frazee
See main entry on page 1

Applesauce See *Rain Makes Applesauce* above for a recipe for homemade applesauce.

Cherries and Cherry Pits

Vera B. Williams
Greenwillow, 1986

Bidemmi is a little girl who loves to write and illustrate with markers. All the stories she writes have something in common—they are all about sharing and eating cherries. Share a bowl of cherries with your students and let them write and illustrate as they eat. Maybe they would also like to plant the cherry pits. *(all ages)*

Cherries

Buy two or three pints of cherries and let the children wash them and remove the stems. When they eat them, remind them to watch out for the cherry pits.

The Tale of Peter Rabbit

Beatrix Potter
Frederick Warne, 1902

This well-known and well-loved book about Flopsy, Mopsy, Cottontail, and Peter is familiar to many children. If your students do not know Peter Rabbit, be sure to share this delightful story with them while they eat bread, milk, and blackberries like the three good little rabbits—Flopsy, Mopsy, and Cottontail. *(all ages)*

Bread, Milk, and Blackberries

Bake some bread (see recipe listed with *The Little Red Hen* or *The Giant Jam Sandwich*, pages 16–17) or enjoy a good crusty bakery bread. Let the children wash some blackberries, put them in a bowl, and eat them covered with milk.

The First Strawberries

Retold by Joseph Bruchac • Illustrated by Anna Vojtech
Dial, 1993

The First Strawberries is a Cherokee story about how strawberries first came into the world. In the beginning, the great Creator made a man and a woman. They marry and are happy together for a long time. One day following a quarrel, the woman leaves home in anger. The sun tires to help get the couple back together by sending several types of berries to Earth. Not until strawberries are sent does the woman notice. As she picks berries for her husband, he comes to her, and each is forgiven. Even today when the Cherokee people eat strawberries, they are reminded that "friendship and respect are as sweet as the taste of ripe, red berries." *(all ages)*

Fresh Strawberries

Serve fresh, sweet strawberries. If possible visit a strawberry field and have the children pick them fresh. What could be simpler?

The Little Mouse, the Red Ripe Strawberry, and the Big Hungry Bear

Don and Audrey Wood • Illustrated by Don Wood
Child's Play, 1984

How would you hide a red, ripe, juicy strawberry from a big hungry bear? *(ps, pm)*

Fresh Strawberries

If strawberries are available locally, arrange a field trip to go strawberry picking. If this is not possible, buy them at the grocery store. Let the children carefully wash them and eat them. You might even want to have a funny-nose-and-glasses disguise to wear while you eat them. Watch out for the big hungry bear!

Curly-Locks

Traditional Mother Goose

Curly-locks, curly-locks
Wilt thou be mine?
Thou shall not wash dishes
Nor yet feed the swine;

But sit on a cushion
And sew a fine seam
And feed upon strawberries,
Sugar and cream.

Strawberries and Cream

- 2–3 pints of strawberries
- 2 pints heavy cream

- powdered sugar

Have children wash and slice the strawberries and put them in a bowl. Mix cream with the strawberries and serve in individual bowls. Sprinkle with powdered sugar if desired. Sit on a cushion and enjoy!

The Relatives Came

Cynthia Rylant • Illustrated by Stephen Gammell
Bradbury, 1985 ★ Caldecott Honor Book

This book details the excitement and activities of a family reunion. One thing most families do when they get together is eat. This family eats up all the strawberries and melons. Your class will enjoy cutting and serving strawberries and watermelon. You might also introduce several additional kinds of melon. *(all ages)*

Strawberries and Melons

You'll need strawberries, watermelon, cantaloupe, muskmelon and honeydew melon. Have the children help cut up the fruit and arrange the pieces on a serving tray or in a bowl.

The Day It Rained Watermelons

Mabel Watts • Illustrated by Lee Anderson
E. M. Hale, 1967

Farmer O'Dell gets up on the wrong side of the bed one day and gets a late start for the market. As he hurries down bumpy roads with his truck full of watermelons, the melons tumble out the back. He doesn't discover this until he arrives at the market with only three left to sell. What will he do now? *(ps, pm)*

Watermelon

Buy a watermelon and, taking care not to lose it out the back of your car, bring it to school. Let the children help you slice it up for a refreshing snack. You might want to buy a yellow watermelon for the children to try.

Cantaloupes

Traditional Mother Goose

Cantaloupes! Cantaloupes!
What is the price?
Eight for a dollar,
And all very nice.

Cantaloupes

Bring a cantaloupe or two to school. Help children cut the melons into wedges or small pieces.

Oranges

Zack Rogow • Illustrated by Mary Szilagyi
Orchard Books, 1988

The book begins with a farmer plowing the earth and planting seeds and ends with a child eating a ripe, juicy orange. In between, the life of an orange tree and the process of harvesting oranges is simply described. *(ps, pm)*

Fresh Oranges

After reading this book, share fresh, juicy oranges with the children.

"Bananas and Cream"
from Every Time I Climb a Tree

David McCord, Illustrated by Marc Simont
Little, Brown, 1925

In *Every Time I Climb a Tree* you will find the poem "Bananas and Cream." Like the children in the poem, all your students will yell for after hearing this poem is *bananas and cream!* *(all ages)*

Bananas and Cream

For each child you will need:

- 1 banana
- ½ cup milk or cream

Let each child peel and slice the banana. Pour in the milk and enjoy.

Fiesta!

Beatriz McConnie Zapater • Illustrated by José Ortega
Simon & Schuster, 1992

Latin American customs are celebrated through dance, costumes, food, and music. *Fiesta!* explains some of the Hispanic holidays celebrated by Chucho, his sister Maria, and his parents. One of Chucho's favorite foods from Columbia is pantacones, also called tostones, or fried plantain. *(all ages)*

Pantacones or Fried Plantains

- 2 medium firm plantains
- ½ teaspoon ginger
- 1 teaspoon salt
- ¾ cup oil

Peel plantains. Cut in half lengthwise and remove seeds. Cut into cubes. Combine ginger and salt. Roll cubes in spices to coat them. Heat oil in a skillet. Fry ⅓ of plantain at a time in hot oil until well browned. Drain on paper towels. Serve hot or cooled.

This Is the Way We Eat Our Lunch

Edith Bauer • Illustrated by Steve Bjorkman
See main entry on page 1

Fried Plantain

- 1 very firm plantain* per child
- 1 tablespoon butter, per child
- brown sugar
- ground nutmeg

Have the children peel their plantain and cut it in half. Melt butter in frying pan; add plantain and cook over low heat until they are tender. Stir carefully. The children can sprinkle them with brown sugar and nutmeg. Serve hot.

*Firm bananas can be substituted for plantain.

Three Days on a River in a Red Canoe

Vera B. Williams
Greenwillow, 1981 ★ A Reading Rainbow Book

If you are fortunate enough to take your class on a camping trip, making these recipes outside will make cooking more authentic. If a camping trip isn't possible, maybe you could make this at a national, state or city park. If you want to make it indoors, I would suggest setting up a tent and "camp ground" on your school grounds. *(all ages)*

Fruit Stew and Dumplings

A recipe for fruit stew and dumplings is included in this book.

More recipes for this book on page 64.

Banbury Fair

Traditional Mother Goose

As I was going to Banbury,
Upon a summer's day,
My dame had butter, eggs, and fruit,
And I had corn and hay.

Jack drove the ox, and Tom the swine,
Dick took the foal and mare;
I sold them all—then home to dine
From famous Banbury fair.

Fruit

Have several kinds of fruit available for the children to sample, or mix them all together for a fruit salad. You may wish to include apples, bananas, kiwi, oranges, muskmelon, honeydew melon, pears, pineapple, grapes, cantaloupe and watermelon

Mr. Rabbit and the Lovely Present

Charlotte Zolotow • Illustrated by Maurice Sendak
Harper and Row, 1962 ★ Caldecott Honor Book

When a little girl cannot decide what to give her mother for her birthday, she receives the help of a rabbit. After much discussion, a perfect present is found. *(all ages)*

Fruit Salad

Use apples, bananas, grapes and pears for this salad. Ask each child to bring in a piece of fruit from the story. Have a basket available for the children to leave the fruit in when they arrive at school. When it's time to make the fruit salad, each child can wash and prepare the fruit they brought.

The Carrot Seed

Ruth Krauss
Harper, 1945

A little boy plants a carrot seed and remains undaunted as all the members of his family tell him it will never grow. *(all ages)*

Carrots

You will need one carrot per child. Have each child clean and slice one carrot. Put half the slices in a bowl and half in a cooking pot. Boil or steam the carrots until tender. The children can taste and compare the raw and cooked carrots. You can also bring a fresh carrot that still has its leafy top to show children what carrots look like as they grow.

Beach Bunny

Jennifer Selby
Harcourt Brace, 1995

Beach Bunny is a colorfully illustrated story about Harold, a young rabbit, and his mother. They enjoy a day at the beach full of swimming, fishing and shelling. They also enjoy a picnic lunch. *(ps, pm)*

Carrot-Raisin Salad

You could make the traditional shredded carrot and raisin salad that is available on most restaurant salad bars. But for a change you may want to try this sweeter salad.

- 1 lb. carrots
- 1 cup mini marshmallows
- ½ cup cubed pineapple
- ½ cup raisins
- ½ cup coconut
- 1 cup mayonnaise
- 1 cup whipped cream

Have the children peel carrots and shred them on a cheese grater or with a potato peeler until you get about 3½ cups of shredded carrots. Add marshmallows, pineapple, coconut and raisins. Pour mayonnaise in and mix. Fold in whipped cream.

More recipes for this book on page 116.

The Enormous Turnip

Traditional Fairy Tale

In this fairy tale, a farmer grows an enormous turnip. It is so large that he needs the help of his wife, a little girl, a little boy, and several animals to pull it up! *(all ages)*

Turnips

You will need about 1 pound of fresh turnips. Peel off the waxy skin. Cut into 1-inch cubes. Put them into a pot and cover with water. Boil turnips 8 to 10 minutes or until tender. Salt and pepper to taste. Serve with butter. Many children have never tasted turnips before, and it is surprising the number who will ask for seconds.

The Vanishing Pumpkin

Tony Johnson • Illustrated by Tomie dePaola
G. P. Putnam, 1983

A 700-year-old woman and an 800-year-old man go as fast as they can—"in fact they fairly flew"—in search of the pumpkin that was snitched from their garden. Many children do not realize that pumpkin for their pumpkin pies does not just come out of a can. Cook a pumpkin to taste or to use in a pumpkin pie recipe. *(all ages)*

Cooked Pumpkin

Be sure you buy a cooking pumpkin and not a pumpkin grown strictly for decorating purposes. Cut open the pumpkin and clean out all the seeds and strings. Cut the shell into pieces. Steam the pumpkin pieces by placing them in a steamer or metal strainer. Put the steamer on the bottom of a large pot and add water just to the bottom. Steam the pieces in a covered pot for 30 to 45 minutes or until the pumpkin is soft. Peel the rind from the pumpkin pulp. Put pumpkin pulp through a food mill or blender until smooth. Use as you would canned pumpkin.

Too Many Tamales

Gary Soto • Illustrated by Ed Martinez
See main entry on page 24

Pumpkin Seeds

- pumpkin seeds
- salt
- vegetable oil

Wash pumpkin pulp from seeds. Steam seeds for half an hour to soften. Pat dry. Spread seeds on a cookie sheet. Sprinkle with a little oil. Salt to taste. Bake for half an hour at 300°.

Chop, Simmer, Season

Alexa Brandenberg
Harcourt Brace, 1997

Simple text describes the action as the characters prepare food in their kitchen. *(ps)*

Garden Greens

Plan a salad with your class using fresh garden greens. Ask each child to bring in a different green to help prepare the meal. If possible, visit a garden or farm to buy the greens. Use greens that might not be familiar to your children: endive, escarole, bib lettuce, romaine, and others.

More recipes for this book on pages 47 and 92.

D.W. the Picky Eater

Marc Brown
Little, Brown, 1995

Arthur's little sister D.W. is a picky eater and won't eat anything with "eyes, pickles, or tomatoes, mushrooms, pineapples, parsnips and cauliflower." She won't eat liver and more than anything else, she hates spinach! When D.W. wants to join the family at Grandma Thora's birthday celebration, she has to agree to eat something from the menu. She orders and loves her choice—Little Bo Beep Pot Pie—but is in for a big surprise when she finds out what is in it! *(ps, pm)*

Little Bo Peep Pot Pie *(really Spinach Pie)*

- pie pastry to line bottom of 9" pie pan and to cover top of pie
- 1 pound fresh spinach
- 1 tablespoon butter
- 3 eggs

- 1 cup small curd cottage cheese
- 5 tablespoons milk
- ½ cup Parmesan cheese
- salt and pepper to taste

Line pie pan with dough and bake for 10 minutes at 375°. Wash fresh spinach well. Steam spinach just until leaves wilt. Drain well. Chop spinach and mix with butter. In separate bowl, break eggs and then add cottage cheese, Parmesan cheese, milk and seasonings. Add spinach to mixture. Spread in pie crust. Cover with crust and bake about 35 minutes at 350° or until pie crust is browned and inside is cooked.

When I Was Young in the Mountains

Cynthia Rylant • Illustrated by Diane Goode
E. P. Dutton, 1982
★ Reading Rainbow Selection ★ Caldecott Honor Book

This is a delightful book about earlier times and life in the mountains. Your students can compare shopping at a general store, baptisms in the river, and using a "johnny-house" at night to lifestyles we are accustomed to today. And many children will not have tasted okra. You can buy it frozen at the grocery store if you cannot find it fresh for the recipe below. *(all ages)*

Okra

Wash 3 or 4 okra; cut off stems. Cut 1-inch pieces and put into ½ to ¾ cup boiling water. Simmer about 5 minutes or until tender. Do not overcook. Drain. Salt, pepper and butter to taste.

American Too

Elisa Barone • Illustrated by Ted Lewin
Lothrop, Lee & Shepard, 1996

This book is based on a true story about Rosie's arrival to America from Italy. The Italian American culture is shared as Rosie tries to become more American. This is an excellent book to share when discussing immigration and the blending of cultures.

Eggplant

- 1–2 eggplants
- salt
- olive oil

Slice the eggplant into ¼-inch slices. Sprinkle both sides of slices with salt. Place in a long cooking pan or in a colander. Set the eggplant aside for about an hour allowing it to drain. Rinse with cold water and pat dry. Brush with olive oil and grill on a barbecue grill or in a skillet with a little olive oil. Serve hot.

More recipes for this book on page 23.

Tight Times

Barbara Shook Hazen • Illustrated by Trina Schart Hyman
Viking, 1979 ★ Reading Rainbow Selection

When Dad loses his job and the family goes through "tight times," they find they have to cut back on some of the things they are used to. They eat Mr. Bulk cereal, instead of cereal in little boxes, and they go to the sprinkler instead of the beach. Instead of eating roast beef, they now eat "soupy things with lima beans." After reading *Tight Times*, serve lima beans in class. You can buy frozen limas, or buy the dry limas and make them from scratch. *(ps, pm)*

Lima Beans

- 12-oz. bag of dried lima beans

Sort beans and discard any that look bad. Then place in a large cooking pot and cover with water to soak overnight. The next day, add more water if needed and boil. Turn down the heat and simmer in a covered pot for approximately ½ hour or until tender. Serve with butter.

Alexander and the Terrible, Horrible, No Good, Very Bad Day

Judith Viorst • Illustrated by Ray Cruz
Atheneum, 1984 ★ Reading Rainbow Selection

On this terrible day, nothing goes right for poor Alexander. There's kissing on TV, and he hates kissing. There's lima beans for dinner, and he hates lima beans.

When children help prepare food, they will usually taste what they cook. They may surprise you—and even themselves—by liking lima beans! *(all ages)*

Lima Beans

If you want to cook dried lima beans, refer to the recipe listed under *Tight Times* above. If you prefer a quicker method, buy a bag of frozen beans and cook according to directions .

The Boy Who Ate the Flowers

Nancy Sherman • Illustrated by Nancy Carroll
Platt and Munk, 1960

This book is featured in the introduction and was one of the first books in my collection as a child. Told in rhymed couplets, it is the story of a boy who loves to eat flowers. His parents worry, but are advised by their doctor that he will soon bore of eating flowers. A French chef is hired by the family and he serves the boy Tulip Pie, Petunia Stew and Forsythia Fricassee, among other floral delicacies. One day the boy does tire of eating flowers and requests oatmeal.

Because the flowers enjoyed by the young boy in the book are not all edible, I have included a recipe for fried zucchini blossoms. Although this recipe may sound odd, zucchini blossoms are popular in some finer Italian restaurants. If you want a more traditional meal, you may want to make the oatmeal found on page 6. *(ps, pm)*

Fried Zucchini Blossoms

- 6 fresh zucchini blossoms
- 1 tablespoon flour
- 2 teaspoons olive oil
- salt and pepper

Rinse blossoms and shake off excess water. Place blossoms and flour in a large plastic bag and shake gently to coat. Fry blossoms in olive oil just until wilted. Serve warm with salt and pepper to taste.

The Pumpkin Man from Piney Creek

Darleen Bailey Beard • Illustrated by Laura Keller
Simon & Schuster, 1995

Hattie's father is selling his crop to the Pumpkin Man, but Hattie still hopes she'll be able to keep one pumpkin for a jack-o'-lantern and another for her mother's blue ribbon pies. When Hattie hides a perfect pumpkin, Pa tells her he has promised the Pumpkin Man one hundred pumpkins and must keep his promise. How does this problem get solved?

You may want to make Ma's blue ribbon pie using the recipe included at the end of the story, or the beans and cornbread (page 20) that Hattie's family eats for supper. *(pm, in)*

Beans

- 1 cup dry navy beans
- 1 8-oz. can tomato sauce
- 1 tablespoon molasses
- 1 tablespoon maple syrup
- ½ teaspoon salt
- 2 tablespoons mustard
- 2 tablespoons ketchup
- 1 small onion, chopped
- 1 tablespoon oil

Wash and soak beans overnight. Drain water. Brown onions in oil. Combine all ingredients. Place in a casserole dish, cover and bake at 350° for 2½ to 3 hours.

The Sugaring Off Party

Jonathon London • Illustrated by Giles Pelletier
See main entry on page 9

Baked Beans

Be sure to try to use *real* maple syrup.

- 1 quart parboiled navy beans
- ¼ pound salt pork or bacon
- 1 cup *real* maple syrup
- 1 teaspoon salt

- ¼ teaspoon dry mustard
- dash of pepper
- 1 onion
- boiling water

Put ½ the beans in a casserole dish or bean pot. Cut up salt pork and add to beans. Add the rest of the beans. Mix ½ cup syrup with salt, dry mustard, pepper, and diced onion. Add to beans. Fill the pot with the boiling water. Cover and bake for 4 hours in a 300° oven. Add the other ½ cup of syrup, bake uncovered for an additional 45 minutes to an hour, adding water if necessary.

A Day at Damp Camp

George Ella Lyon • Illustrated by Peter Catalanotto
Orchard Books, 1996

A day at camp is told with simple pairs of rhyming words and beautiful illustrations. Dinnertime is simply stated "Brier Fire, Bean Scene, Own Stone." *(all ages)*

Baked Beans

No doubt the beans eaten at Damp Camp were canned beans heated on the camp fire. Open single-serving cans of beans, one per child, heat and eat. If you want to get a bit more elaborate try adding ingredients to make a baked bean casserole. See the baked bean recipe above.

Red Bird

Barbara Mitchell • Illustrated by Todd L. W. Doney
See main entry on page 25

Spicy Beans

- 1 teaspoon olive oil
- 1 small onion, diced

- 2 tablespoons chili powder
- 2 cans pinto beans or 1 lb. dry beans soaked overnight and drained

Saute onion in oil until tender. Add beans and chili powder. Heat and serve with fry bread (p.25).

The Tortilla Factory

Gary Paulsen • Illustrated Ruth Wright Paulsen
See main entry on page 25

Bean Filling

- 1 can refried beans or 1 can chili beans run through a food processor
- ½ teaspoon garlic powder
- 1 teaspoon onion powder

Combine all ingredients and use to fill tortillas (p. 25).

The Vegetable Show

Laurie Krasny Brown
Little, Brown, 1995

This book talks about nutrition and eating well. String beans, peas, mashed potatoes, fries, pancakes, rutabagas and carrot juice are some of the foods mentioned. You may want to prepare fresh string beans, canned beans and frozen beans to let children compare the tastes and textures of each. The same can be done with peas. Children will also enjoy making *real* mashed potatoes. *(all ages)*

Mashed Potatoes

- You will need a potato peeler and 1 potato per child.

Have the children peel potatoes with adult supervision. Quarter the potatoes and boil in water until tender. Drain water. Using a hand potato masher, allow each child to mash the potatoes Add 2 tablespoons of butter (optional) and ¼ cup of milk. Beat potatoes with hand mixer until soft and fluffy, adding more milk if necessary. Serve hot.

The Potato Man

Megan McDonald, Illustrated by Ted Lewin
Orchard Books, 1991

Grandpa shares his memories of a time when knife sharpeners, organ grinders and vegetable vendors came to town. He tells the story of Mr. Angelo, the Potato Man, who had lost his right eye in the Great War. All the children feared him and made fun of him until one Christmas Day. *(all ages)*

Peeled Potatoes

- You will need a potato peeler and 1 potato per child.

With adult supervision, allow each child to peel a potato with the potato peeler. Have them cut their potato into quarters. Boil potato pieces in a sauce pan until tender. Serve hot with butter.

Jamie O'Rourke and the Big Potato

Tomie dePaola

Putnam, 1992

In this Irish tale, Jamie O'Rourke is the laziest man in all of Ireland. He does all he can to get out of work, especially if it means growing potatoes. When his wife gets hurt, he's afraid he will go hungry. When he meets up with a leprechaun he wishes for the largest "partie" in all the world—which is exactly what he gets! The potato grows so large he can't get it out of the ground without help. When the potato gets stuck between the fences, he needs the townspeople's help to eat it all. *(all ages)*

Potatoes

Buy the largest potatoes you can find and serve them in a variety of ways— mashed, boiled, fried, baked, and hash browned. Have a potato tasting party.

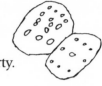

One Potato

Sue Porter

Bradbury, 1989

When only one potato remains, pig, goat, sheep, goose and cow decide to hold a competition to see who will get to eat it. Goat tries his hardest to rig the contest so he can have the last potato all to himself. When he "wins," he discovers the potato is gone—to a family of mice who share *one potato!* *(ps, pm)*

Baked Potato

Pair children up with a partner. You will need one medium baking potato per pair. Have the children scrub their potatoes and wrap them in aluminum foil. Bake at 350° for 45 minutes to an hour. Cut in half and let each child enjoy half a potato with butter, sour cream or cheese.

The Old, Old Man and the Very Little Boy

Kristine L. Franklin • Illustrated by Terea Shaffer

Atheneum, 1992

Set in Africa, a very little boy visits an old, old man of the village bringing him roasted sweet potatoes. The old, old man shares the stories of his youth while the boy doubts the old man was ever young. Soon both grow old—the old man dies and the very little boy has a family of his own. As he grows old, the young children of the village beg him to tell stories of his youth. They too, doubt that he could ever have been young. *(all ages)*

Roasted Sweet Potato

You'll need 1 sweet potato per child. Prick several fork holes in potato skins. Bake at 375° for 45 to 60 minutes or until tender. Allow potatoes to cool and eat them right out of the skins.

Seven Candles for Kwanzaa

Andrea Davis Pinkney • Illustrated by Brian Pinkney
Dial Books for Young Readers, 1993

This book provides a simple explanation of Kwanzaa, making it easy for young children to understand. The illustrations are colorful and very appealing. After reading the book with your class enjoy making collard greens together. *(all ages)*

Collard Greens

- 1 or 2 ham hocks, or a ham butt
- 3–4 pounds fresh collard greens
- 2 tablespoons bacon fat
- ⅓ teaspoon sugar
- ½ teaspoon salt

Place ham hocks or ham butt in a large pot. Put in enough water to cover. Wash fresh collard greens thoroughly. Trim off thick, tough stems. Cut leaves into small, fine pieces. Be sure there is at least 3½ cups of water left in the pot, if not, add some. Add remaining ingredients to pot. Bring to a boil then simmer for an hour, stirring once or twice. After an hour, remove lid, turn up heat and allow to cook until there is only about an inch of water in the bottom of the pan.

Roasted Yams   See Roasted Sweet Potato recipe on page 82.

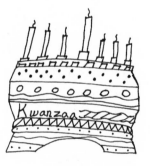

Cookies, Candy

The Doorbell Rang

Pat Hutchins
Greenwillow, 1986

There are twelve cookies for Victoria and Sam to share, until the doorbell rings. Each time the doorbell rings, more visitors come and the cookies must be divided up among all the company. All goes well until twelve friends are gathered at the table and the doorbell rings. What will they do? They have no more cookies to divide!

When you make these chocolate chip cookies, be sure to make a few extra in case someone shows up at your door. *(all ages)*

Chocolate Chip Cookies

- ¼ cup brown sugar
- ½ cup sugar
- ½ cup shortening
- 1 egg, beaten
- 2 teaspoons vanilla

- 1 cup flour
- ¾ teaspoon baking soda
- ½ teaspoon salt
- 3 ozs. chopped nuts
- 1 cup chocolate chips

Cream the sugars with the shortening. Stir in egg and vanilla. Combine dry ingredients; add to sugar-shortening mixture. Add nuts and chocolate chips. Bake on a lightly greased cookie sheet for 8 to 10 minutes in preheated 350° oven. Makes about 3 dozen.

"Cookies" from Frog and Toad Together

Arnold Lobel
Harper and Row, 1972
★ Newbery Honor Book ★ Reading Rainbow Selection

In the story "Cookies," Toad makes some cookies and takes them over to his friend Frog's house. The cookies are delicious and Frog and Toad have a difficult time controlling the urge to eat them all. *(pm)*

No-Bake Chocolate Chip Cookies

- 4 tablespoons cocoa
- 2 cups sugar
- ½ cup margarine
- ½ cup milk

- ½ cup chopped nuts
- ½ cup peanut butter
- 2 teaspoons vanilla
- 3 cups oatmeal

Combine cocoa, sugar, margarine, and milk in pot. Boil for 3 minutes. Remove from heat and add nuts, peanut butter, vanilla, and oats. Beat until well blended. Drop small amounts of mixture onto aluminum foil.

If You Give a Mouse a Cookie
Laura Joffe Numeroff • Illustrated by Felicia Bond
Harper and Row, 1985

If you give a mouse a cookie he is going to want a glass of milk. What will happen if you give him the milk? You will have to decide whether you will share these cookies with a mouse or not! *(ps, pm)*

Chocolate Chip Cookies

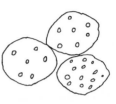

- 1 cup brown sugar
- ½ cup margarine
- 2 tablespoons water
- 1 egg, beaten
- 2 teaspoons vanilla
- ½ teaspoon baking soda
- 1 cup flour
- ½ teaspoon salt
- 6 oz. pkg. chocolate chips

Thoroughly combine sugar and margarine, then add water, egg, and vanilla. Combine with baking soda, flour, and salt. Stir in chocolate chips. Drop dough onto a greased cookie sheet. Bake at 375° for about 10 minutes. Makes about 2 dozen cookies.

Chocolate Chip Cookie Contest
Barbara Douglass
Lothrop, Lee & Shepard, 1985

Kevin plans to enter the Chocolate Chip Cookie Contest at the mall, but he needs to find an adult to help him use the oven. Every adult he asks is too busy to help, but each gives some advice as to what ingredient is missing from his recipe. When he finally finds a grown-up to help him, they make a chocolate chip pizza. Do they win the contest? You be the judge when you make the chocolate chip pizza using the recipe included in the book.

Chocolate Chip Pizza

Have each child bring six of his or her favorite chocolate chip cookies to school. Make the chocolate chip pizza using the recipe in the book and have your own Chocolate Chip Contest. Taste all the different types of cookies. Have a blue ribbon for each child to award to the cookie he or she likes the best. Be sure each child receives a ribbon by creating a variety of categories: biggest, smallest, most chips, etc. This way each will have a ribbon to take home to remember the day's activities.

Cookies
William Jaspersohn
Macmillan, 1993

Did you know that Americans eat 6.5 million pounds of commercially made cookies a day? That is equal to a pound of cookies a month for each person in the United States! Facts about cookies, particularly Famous Amos Cookies, are shared in this nonfiction book. You will visit the Famous Amos Cookie Factory and learn how these famous cookies are made. *(all ages)*

Famous Amos Cookies

Since this book is about Famous Amos Cookies, a brand name available at the grocery store, you should plan to buy the real thing and serve them with milk in your classroom. If your children are set on making cookies, use the recipe on page 85, and add ½ cup of nuts.

If I Could Be My Grandmother
Steven Kroll • Illustrated by Lady McCrady
Pantheon, 1977

What would you do if you were a grandmother? The little girl in this book role plays all the things she would do. She would bake cookies and have cornflakes for breakfast. Find out what your students would do if they were grandparents. *(ps, pm)*

Cookies

- 1 pkg. cake mix, any flavor
- 2 eggs
- ½ cup cooking oil
- 2 tablespoons water

Combine ingredients and mix well. Drop batter by the spoonful onto a greased cookie sheet. Bake for 9 minutes at 350°.

Aunt Flossie's Hat (and Crab Cakes Later)
Elizabeth Fitzgerald Howard • Illustrated by James Ransome
Clarion, 1991

On Sundays, Susan and Sarah visit with their Great-Great Aunt Flossie. They love her house crowded with books, lamps, pictures, pillows and boxes and boxes and boxes of hats. As the girls try on Aunt Flossie's hats, she shares stories and memories that each hat represents. *(all ages)*

Tea and Cookies

When listening to Aunt Flossie's stories and trying on all her hats, Susan and Sarah have tea and cookies. Serve tea and cookies while the children try on hats. Try to imagine where each hat has been worn before.

More recipes for this book on page 61.

Mr. Cookie Baker
Monica Wellington
Dutton, 1992

Mr. Baker bakes his delicious cookies every morning and decorates them with colored sprinkles just in time for the arrival of all the hungry children. The cookies get sold and the shop closes for the night. This simple text is accompanied by bright, colorful illustrations that appeal to young children. Making the cookies will appeal to them even more! *(ps, pm)*

Cookie Recipe

Use the cookie recipe included in the back of *Mr. Cookie Baker*. For easy sugar cookies, make them from pre-made refrigerator cookie dough from the store. Be sure to include lots of choices for sprinkles to decorate the cookies after baking.

The Baker's Dozen
Retold by Aaron Shepard • Illustrated by Wendy Edelson
Atheneum, 1995

This colonial tale shares the legend of how a baker's dozen, 13 instead of 12 cookies, came to be. A greedy baker is visited by a mysterious women who helps him see that giving more than is expected is rewarded. *(pm, in)*

Gingerbread Cookies (shape like Santa)

- ⅓ cup shortening
- ¾ cup brown sugar, packed
- 1½ cups dark molasses
- ⅔ cup cold water
- 7 cups flour
- 1½ teaspoons baking soda
- 1 teaspoon salt
- 1 teaspoon allspice
- 1 teaspoon ginger
- 1 teaspoon cloves
- 1 teaspoon cinnamon

Cream shortening until it gets soft. Add sugar and molasses. Mix in water. Add dry ingredients. Refrigerate for 2 hours.

On a floured surface, roll dough until it is ½ inch thick. Use a Santa Claus-shaped cookie cutter to cut out cookies. Place on greased cookie sheet. Bake at 350° for 15 minutes. When cool, decorate with red and white icing to look like Santa Claus. Tubes of icing can be purchased in the baking section of the grocery store.

The Gingerbread Doll
Susan Tews • Illustrated by Megan Lloyd
Clarion, 1993

While baking Christmas cookies, Great Grandma Rebecca recalls the Christmas of 1930. During the depression, when Rebecca was a young girl, she remembers being terribly poor, yet hoping she would find a porcelain doll under the Christmas tree. Though the porcelain doll was not there that year, her mother made her a gingerbread doll. Rebecca used green fabric and buttons and made her doll a dress. She named her Button Marie. As the years went by and times got better, Rebecca would receive many wonderful dolls including a cornhusk doll, a store bought cloth doll and even the porcelain doll. But great grandma always kept the scrap cloth and buttons that once belonged to Button Marie. As she shares these memories of Christmas, she brings out the buttons and dress that belonged to Button Marie to show the children. *(pm, in)*

Gingerbread Cookies

See the recipe under *The Gingerbread Man* for a great gingerbread cookie recipe. Instead of shaping the dough like Play-Doh, roll out the cookie dough and use a large gingerbread man or woman cookie cutter to make the cookies. Allow the children to use fabric to make a gingerbread doll like in the story. These would make great gifts to take to a nursing home or hospital for the holidays.

The Gingerbread Man
Retold and illustrated by Paul Galdone
Houghton Mifflin, 1975

In this familiar tale, the gingerbread man gets chased through the countryside by the little old woman, the little old man, and many others. This recipe for gingerbread men is great because you don't have to roll out the dough. Give each child a little ball and have them mold it as they would clay. You do have to watch the cookies carefully while they bake, as children won't make them a consistent thickness. Some may tend to burn while others are not quite ready. Check often, using the time given very generally. *(all ages)*

Gingerbread Men

- 1 cup brown sugar
- ¾ cup shortening
- 1 egg
- ¼ cup molasses
- 2 cups flour

- 1 teaspoon ground ginger
- ½ teaspoon allspice
- 1 teaspoon baking soda
- 2 teaspoons cinnamon
- raisins for eyes

Combine sugar and shortening. Mix in egg and molasses. Combine dry ingredients in separate bowl, then combine with dough mixture. Refrigerate for 20 minutes.

Give each child a piece of aluminum foil and let them shape the cookie dough as they would modeling clay. Provide raisins or red hot candies for eyes, mouth, and buttons, if you desire. Bake at 350° for about 10 minutes; allow more time for the thicker cookie pieces and less time for the thin ones. Let cookies cool slightly before removing them from the pan. They may be decorated with icing after cooling if you desire. Doesn't your kitchen smell good? Icing can be purchased in tubes in the baking area of the grocery store.

The Gingerbread Man
Retold by Jim Aylesworth • Illustrated by Barbara McClintock
Scholastic, 1998

This traditional tale is retold by a present-day author. Children love to read about the famous cookie who "runs and runs as fast as he can." Hopefully the children will be able to enjoy some gingerbread people before they run away. *(all ages)*

Gingerbread Men/Women

Using the recipe on page 88, have the children shape the cookies like modeling clay, or roll them out on a floured surface and use cookie cutters to create a variety of gingerbread people. There is also a recipe for gingerbread cookies included in *The Gingerbread Man*.

The Lion, the Witch and the Wardrobe

C. S. Lewis
Macmillan, 1953

This is the first of seven books written about the magical land of Narnia. Lucy, Susan, and Peter must rescue their brother, Edmund, from the alluring and wicked White Witch, who tempts him with the sweetness of Turkish Delight. *(pm, in)*

Turkish Delight

- 2 tablespoons water
- ⅔ cup fruit pectin
- ½ teaspoon baking soda
- 1 cup corn syrup, light
- ¾ cup sugar
- 2 tablespoons frozen orange juice concentrate, thawed

- ¼ cup raspberry jelly
- 1 tablespoon lemon juice
- ½ cup chopped nuts

In a large pot, stir water and pectin together. Add baking soda (the mixture will foam). In a second pan, combine corn syrup and sugar. Heat the ingredients in both pans. Heat the pectin until the foam has stopped and heat the sugar solution until it boils. As the sugar boils, pour in the pectin. Stir in orange juice and jelly for 1 minute. Remove from heat and add lemon juice and nuts. Pour into an 8-inch square pan. Let stand for several hours at room temperature until firm. Sprinkle with powdered sugar.

Handy Pandy

Traditional Mother Goose

Handy Pandy, Jack-a-dandy,
Loves plum cake and sugar candy.
He bought some at the grocer's shop
And out he came, hop, hop, hop.

Sugar Candy

- 2 cups sugar
- ½ teaspoon cinnamon

- 4½ cups nuts (pecans, walnuts)
- 1 cup water

Combine all ingredients in an electric skillet. Heat until liquid evaporates. Place nuts on a baking sheet and divide into bite-sized pieces. Cool.

"Stout's Candy" from The Giant's Farm

Jane Yolen • Illustrated by Tomie dePaola

Seabury Press, 1977

This book contains five short stories about five giants who live together on a farm. In "Stout's Candy," Stout, the fattest of the giants, wants to make candy. He soon discovers that though he has all the ingredients, he doesn't have any tsp. or tbsp. or a c. as called for in the recipe. Dab, the smallest giant, explains that tsp. means teaspoon, tbsp. is tablespoon, and c. stands for cup. Stout is now happy, as he can make his no-bake candy. *(ps, pm)*

Stout's Giant No-Cook Bon Bons

The recipe for Stout's Giant No-Cook Bon Bons is included in *The Giant's Farm*. The children will be as happy as Stout when they try this candy.

Jelly Beans for Breakfast

Mariam Young • Illustrated by Beverly Komoda

Parents' Magazine Press, 1968

We will have all the fun in the world at my house, including ride our bikes to the moon, play gypsies, have beds made of twigs covered with moss, and for breakfast— we will have jelly beans! *(ps, pm)*

Jelly Beans

A bag or two of jelly beans will delight your students when you pretend that you are eating them for breakfast. Serve with orange juice to create a breakfast atmosphere.

Hansel and Gretel

Retold by Rika Lesser • Illustrated by Paul Zelinsky

Dodd, Mead, 1984 ★ Caldecott Honor Book

This Caldecott Honor Book is illustrated with great detail. Your students will enjoy making a miniature candy house. *(all ages)*

Candy House

- 6 graham crackers per child
- 1 empty half-pint milk carton per child

Frosting Cement

- 2 egg whites
- ½ teaspoon cream of tartar
- 2 cups powdered sugar

Beat the egg whites and the cream of tartar until stiff. Add the powdered sugar and beat 5 more minutes with an electric mixer. This frosting can be used to cement your candy house together, and it will harden when it dries. Using graham crackers and the frosting, let your students cement the crackers to the half-pint milk carton for the base of the house. Cement candies on the cube with the cement frosting to look like a candy house. These work well: small hard candies, such as red hots, M&Ms, Reese's Pieces, Life Savers, colorful cereals, peppermint candies, gumdrops, cookie sprinkles, chocolate chips, or mini marshmallows.

The Hungry Thing

Jan Sleplan and Ann Seidler • Illustrated by Richard E. Martin
Scholastic, 1967

When the Hungry Thing asks for feetloaf, and a fanana, your children will quickly figure out what he is hungry for. You might want to buy a bag of gollipops—I mean lollipops—or you may want to make your own. *(all ages)*

"Gollipops"

- 36 lollipop sticks
- ½ cup butter
- 1½ cups sugar
- 1 cup light corn syrup
- food coloring
- peppermint flavoring

Grease a cookie sheet or line it with waxed paper. Arrange sticks on cookie sheet, leaving lots of space between them. Combine butter, sugar, and corn syrup in a pan. Heat mixture until it starts to boil. Cook on medium heat, stirring occasionally, until it reaches 270° on a candy thermometer. (Be sure to use extreme caution around this hot liquid.) Remove from heat. Add food coloring and flavoring. Quickly spoon candy over sticks, keeping candy as round as you can. Remove from cookie sheet when cooled completely.

Chocolate Fever

Robert Kimmel Smith
Dell, 1972

Charlie and the Chocolate Factory

Roald Dahl
Bantam Skylark, 1964

The Chocolate Touch

Patrick Skene Catling
Bantam, Skylark, 1952

After reading these books, buy each child a chocolate bar or small chocolate candies. If you prefer, you might even want to make chocolate candies. You will need candy molds and chocolate pieces, both available at candy stores or hobby and craft stores. *(all are pm, in)*

Cakes, Tarts

Chop, Simmer, Season
Alexa Brandenberg
See main entry on page 47

Strawberry Layer Cake

- 1 pkg. strawberry cake mix
- 2 pkgs. frozen strawberries, thawed
- 2 pkgs. frozen non-dairy topping, thawed
- fresh strawberries

Prepare cake in two round cake pans using directions on package. When cool, slice layers in half crosswise. To assemble cake, alternate cake layer, non-dairy topping, and strawberries. Frost the sides with topping. Garnish with fresh strawberries. Refrigerate until ready to eat.

Bat, Bat, Come Under My Hat
Traditional Mother Goose

Bat, bat, come under my hat
And I'll give you a slice of bacon;
And when I bake, I'll give you cake
If I am not mistaken.

Raspberry Cake

- 4 eggs
- 1 pkg. white cake mix
- 10-oz. pkg. frozen
  red raspberries, thawed
- 1 pkg. raspberry gelatin
- ⅔ cup oil
- 2 teaspoons raspberry
  flavoring, if available

Combine all ingredients in a large bowl. Mix well. Spread in a well-greased 13x 9-inch baking pan. Bake at 325° for 50 minutes, or until done. Top with whipped cream.

Happy Birthday!
Gail Gibbons
Holiday House, 1986

Gail Gibbons explains many of our birthday traditions in a simple and colorful manner. Of course with this book you will want to bake and decorate a birthday cake! *(ps, pm)*

Lemon Birthday Cake

- 1 pkg. lemon cake mix
- 1 pkg. lemon instant pudding
- 4 eggs, unbeaten
- ¾ cup cooking oil
- ¾ cup water

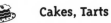
Place all ingredients in bowl and beat until well blended. Grease a 9x13-inch cake pan. Bake for 40 minutes at 350°. Remove the cake from the oven and pierce the entire surface with a fork. While the cake is still hot, pour the following topping over all:

Topping

Mix together 2 cups sifted powdered sugar, ⅓ cup orange juice and 2 tablespoons cooking oil.

Appalachia

Cynthia Rylant • Illustrated by Barry Moser
Harcourt Brace Jovanovich, 1991

Cynthia Rylant's text and Barry Moser's illustrations blend beautifully to describe the gentle, quiet lifestyle and customs of the people who live in Appalachia. *(pm, in)*

Lemon Pound Cake

- ½ cup shortening
- 1 cup butter
- 5 eggs
- 1 cup milk
- 3 cups cake flour
- 3 cups sugar
- ½ teaspoon baking powder
- 1½ teaspoons vanilla
- 2½ teaspoons lemon flavoring

Make sure all ingredients are at room temperature before beginning. Cream butter, shortening and sugar together. Add eggs one at a time, beating as each one is added. Sift the baking powder and cake flour together. Alternately add the dry ingredients, milk and vanilla and lemon extracts to the creamed mixture. Add batter to a greased and floured tube pan. Bake for 1½ hours at 325°. Cool.

More recipes for this book on page 19.

Teddy Bear Baker

Phoebe and Selby Worthington
Puffin, 1979

The teddy bear baker bakes cakes, pies, and breads and delivers them to his friends in town. He enjoys tea and muffins with raspberry jam before going to bed after his full day. The recipe below is for an easy cake, but your children might want to have tea and muffins, or bake a pie or a loaf of bread with the recipes listed elsewhere in *Cook-A-Book*. *(ps, pm)*

Teddy Bear's Cake

- 1 can crushed pineapple
- 2 sticks margarine, cut up and dotted over pie filling
- 1 can cherry pie filling
- 1 yellow cake mix, sprinkled over top

Layer all ingredients in a 9x13-inch pan. Bake at 350° for 55 minutes.

The Duchess Bakes a Cake

Virginia Kahn
Charles Scribner, 1955

When the Duchess becomes bored with her embroidery and tired of talking, she decides to bake a lovely light luscious delectable cake for her family. *(pm)*

Light and Lovely Cake

- 2 cans pie filling, any flavor
- 1 box of yellow cake mix
- 1 stick melted butter
- sprinkle of cinnamon
- chopped nuts, optional

Grease an 8x8-inch cake pan. Put in pie filling. Sprinkle dry cake mix over pie filling. Pour the melted butter on the top. Sprinkle a little cinnamon over all. Add chopped nuts to topping if desired. Bake for 40 minutes at 375°.

Apple Pigs

Ruth Orbach
Philomel, 1981

What would you do if your apple tree produced more apples than you knew what to do with? The girl in this book makes a lot of apple dishes and apple pigs. Directions are given in the book for apple pigs. The recipe for one of the many treats mentioned in the book is given below. *(ps, pm)*

Apple Pan Dowdy

- 4 cups cooking apples
- ¾ cup brown sugar, firmly packed
- ½ cup oatmeal
- ¾ teaspoon cinnamon
- ½ cup flour
- ⅓ cup butter
- ¼ teaspoon allspice

Let the children wash, peel, and slice the apples. Place them into an 8x8-inch greased cake pan. Combine remaining ingredients until crumbly. Evenly spread mixture over the apples. Bake at 350° for 30 to 40 minutes or until top is brown. Serve warm with whipped cream or ice cream.

Queen of Hearts

Traditional Mother Goose

The queen of hearts,
She made some tarts,
All on a summer's day.

The knave of hearts,
He stole those tarts
And took them clean away.

Queen of Hearts Tarts

- refrigerator biscuits
- strawberry jelly

For each child you will need 2 refrigerator biscuits and ½ teaspoon jelly. Using a heart-shaped cookie cutter, let each child cut out 2 heart biscuits. Put ½ teaspoon strawberry jelly between the biscuits. Seal together using fork tines. Bake as directed on the package.

The Missing Tarts

B.G. Hennessy • Illustrated by Tracey Campbell Pearson
Scholastic, 1989

This book begins where "The Queen of Hearts" nursery rhyme ends. After the last verse, in which the Knave of Hearts has stolen the tarts, the queen begins her search. She asks various nursery rhyme characters about the whereabouts of her tarts. *(ps, pm)*

Tarts

- can of sour cherries or blueberries
- 3 tablespoons cornstarch
- ½ cup sugar
- tart shells
- whipped cream or non-dairy whipped topping

Drain fruit, saving the juice. Combine cornstarch and sugar and heat in a pan. Add juice from drained fruit. Add fruit and heat on low until mixture thickens. Cool. Fill purchased tart shells or make graham cracker crusts using the Simple Simon Pie recipe on page 101. Top with whipped topping.

In the Night Kitchen

Maurice Sendak
Harper and Row, 1970 ★ Caldecott Honor Book

In the night kitchen there are all kinds of strange things happening. Mickey awakens and goes to the kitchen, only to find himself in all sorts of adventures. Now, "thanks to Mickey we have cake every morning." *(all ages)*

Morning Coffee Cake

- 1 cup margarine
- 1 cup sugar
- 2 eggs
- 2 teaspoons vanilla
- 1 teaspoon baking soda
- 1½ teaspoons baking powder
- ½ teaspoon salt
- 2 cups flour
- 1 cup sour cream

Filling and topping

- ⅓ cup brown sugar
- 1 cup chopped nuts
- 1/4 cup sugar
- 2 teaspoons cinnamon

In a separate bowl, mix brown sugar, nuts, sugar, and cinnamon for filling and topping. Cream margarine and sugar. Add eggs and vanilla. Beat thoroughly. Add sifted dry ingredients and sour cream alternately in thirds. Spread half of the batter in a greased 9x12-inch pan. Sprinkle half of the filling and topping mixture on top of the batter. Spread on remaining batter and sprinkle remaining filling and topping mixture on the top. Bake at 350° for 35 minutes.

There's a Hippopotamus on Our Roof Eating Cake
Hazel Edwards • Illustrated by Deborah Niland
Holiday House, 1980

There's a hippopotamus on the roof riding his bike, taking a shower, drawing with crayons, and eating cake. The little girl in this book imagines a hippo that does all the things she'd like to do. *(ps, pm)*

Special Cake

- 2 cups sugar
- 2 sticks margarine
- 4 eggs
- 2 teaspoons vanilla

- 1 cup milk
- 1 box graham crackers, crumbled
- 2 cups nuts
- 1 cup crushed pineapple, drained

Combine sugar and margarine; mix in eggs. Add vanilla, milk, and cracker crumbs. Fold in nuts and pineapple. Place in 9x13-inch greased pan and bake at 350° for 45 minutes or until done.

Goody O'Grumpity
Carol Ryrie Brink • Illustrated by Ashley Wolff
North South, 1994

In this 1937 poem, Goody O'Grumpity bakes a cake. All the children and animals stand at Goody's door to lick the dish and smell the wonderful smells that waft from the oven. Illustrator Ashley Wolff sets the story in the Plimouth Plantation where the Pilgrims settled in the mid 1600s. Her linoleum block prints are charming. A recipe for two loaves of spice cake are included at the end of the book. Or you may want to try this one. *(all ages)*

Spice Cake

- ¾ cup butter
- 2 cups brown sugar, firmly packed
- 2 eggs
- 2¾ cups flour
- 1 teaspoon baking soda
- 1 teaspoon cinnamon

- 1 teaspoon cloves
- 1 teaspoon allspice
- 1 teaspoon nutmeg
- 1 teaspoon ginger
- lemon rind
- 1 cup buttermilk

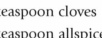

Cream the butter and sugar. Add egg yolks, beating well as you add each one. In a separate bowl blend flour, baking soda and spices. Alternately add dry ingredients and buttermilk to the butter and sugar mixture. Pour into three 8-inch square pans. Bake at 350° for 20 minutes.

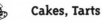
Thunder Cake

Patricia Polacco
Philomel, 1990

To help a young Patricia Polacco overcome her fear of thunderstorms, her grandmother Babushka would bake a Thunder Cake when bad weather threatened. Together they count the seconds between the lightning and thunder to find out how far away the storm is. They need to know this, so they can be sure to have the cake in the oven by the time the storm hits "or it won't be real Thunder Cake." This, like many other Polacco books, is based on the author's memories of her loving grandmother. *(pm, in)*

Thunder Cake   The family recipe for Patricia Polacco's Thunder Cake is included at the end of the story. Enjoy it on a rainy, stormy, thundery day.

Pat-a-Cake

Traditional Mother Goose

Pat-a-cake, pat-a-cake, baker's man,
Bake me a cake as fast as you can.
Pat it and prick it and mark it with a "T,"
And put it in the oven for Tommy and me.

Cake

Using a cake mix from the store, bake it as the directions indicate. Frost the cake using any of the commercially available frostings. After frosting, mark the cake with a T, using red hot candies or M&Ms.

Three Kind Mice

Vivian Sathre • Illustrated by Rodger Wilson
Harcourt Brace, 1997

Three mice make a mess in the kitchen as they prepare a cake from scratch for their friend the cat. Children will enjoy the antics of these kind mice as they prepare for the birthday celebration. *(ps, pm)*

Birthday Cake

- 2 cups dried apples
- ¾ cup sugar
- ⅛ teaspoon salt
- 1 cup flour
- 2 teaspoon cinnamon
- 1 teaspoon baking soda
- ⅛ teaspoon nutmeg
- ¾ cup walnuts, chopped
- 1 egg, beaten
- ½ cup butter, melted

Mix apples and sugar together, let set until sugar dissolves. In a separate bowl, combine salt, flour, cinnamon, baking soda and nutmeg—add to apple mixture. Add egg, butter and walnuts. Put batter into greased 9 x 9-inch pan. Bake in at 350° for 35 to 40 minutes.

Sauce

- 1 cup brown sugar
- 2 tablespoons flour
- ¼ cup butter
- 1 cup water
- 1 teaspoon vanilla

Mix ingredients together in pan and cook until thick. Poke holes in cake and pour sauce over it.

Benny Bakes a Cake

Eve Rice
Greenwillow, 1981

It's Benny's birthday. He and Ralph the dog help Mom bake a birthday cake. While the cake cools, Ralph can't wait any longer and he eats the cake. Benny's disappointed, but Dad saves the celebration with another cake. This cake is so good that your children and the neighborhood dogs might want to eat it before it's cool! *(ps, pm)*

Chocolate Birthday Cake

- 1 pkg. chocolate instant pudding
- 1 pkg. chocolate cake mix
- 4 eggs
- 1 cup water
- ¼ cup cooking oil

Combine the ingredients in a bowl and beat with electric mixer at medium speed for 2 minutes. Grease and flour a bundt pan. Bake at 350° for about an hour, or until a toothpick comes out clean. Cool for 15 minutes and then remove from pan. Continue to cool cake on a rack. Sprinkle with powdered sugar.

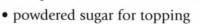

Oh, Lewis!

Eve Rice
Macmillan, 1974

Your students will relate to Lewis as he struggles to keep his winter outerwear zipped, tied, and all in place. After a cold romp in the snow, enjoy hot tea and chocolate cake, as Lewis does. *(ps, pm)*

Chocolate Cake

This is an easy cake to make because you mix all the ingredients right in the cake pan.

- 1½ cups flour
- 1 cup sugar
- 1 teaspoon baking soda
- 1 teaspoon baking powder
- 1 teaspoon salt
- 3 tablespoons unsweetened cocoa powder
- 5 tablespoons oil
- 1 teaspoon vinegar
- 1 teaspoon vanilla
- 1 cup water
- powdered sugar for topping

Combine dry ingredients in an ungreased 8-inch square pan. Make three holes in the mixture. Pour oil in one hole, vinegar in one hole, and vanilla in one hole. Pour water over all and mix with a fork until blended. Bake at 350° for 35 to 40 minutes. Cool and sprinkle with powdered sugar.

More recipes for this book on page 107.

Little Bear Learns to Read the Cookbook
Janice • Illustrated by Marianna
Lothrop, Lee & Shepard, 1969

Little Bear feels as though he cannot do anything. He cannot make milk like the cow, or give eggs like the chicken. He goes to school and learns to read the cookbook. Now he can make the finest chocolate cake ever! *(ps, pm)*

Chocolate Cake

- 1½ cups sugar
- 1⅓ cups flour
- 2 teaspoons baking powder
- 3 tablespoons cocoa
- 1½ teaspoons baking soda
- 1 teaspoon salt
- ½ cup oil
- 1¼ cups milk
- 2 eggs
- 2 teaspoons vanilla

Mix together the sugar, flour, baking powder, cocoa, baking soda, and salt. Add oil, milk, eggs, and vanilla. Pour into a greased 9-inch-square cake pan. Bake for 45 minutes at 350°. Frost if desired.

Just Dessert
Polly Powell
Harcourt Brace, 1996

Patsy has been thinking about the piece of yellow cake with fudge frosting ever since dinner. In the middle of the night she sneaks down to get it only to meet up with a monstrous tiger, a skeleton man and other scary creatures—or so she thinks. She makes it safely back to bed—but she's forgotten something! *(ps, pm)*

Super Yellow Cake with Fudge Frosting

Use a commercial yellow cake mix to make two 9-inch cakes. Cool and remove from cake pans. Frost with canned fudge frosting or use the following recipe.

Fudge Frosting

- 2 ozs. unsweetened chocolate
- ½ cup milk
- 1 cup sugar
- 2 tablespoons butter
- 1 teaspoon vanilla

Melt chocolate in a pan over low heat. After chocolate squares are melted, add sugar and milk. Heat to soft boil stage, or until a small amount will form a soft ball in a glass of cold water. Add remaining ingredients. Let cool a few minutes. Beat until smooth. If frosting is too thick, add a small amount of milk until spreadable.

 # Pies

Down Buttermilk Lane

Barbara Mitchell • Illustrated by John Sandford
Lothrop, Lee & Shepard, 1993

This book follows an Amish family as they ride their buggy into town to run errands. They buy a shoofly pie and enjoy other Amish foods at dinner. The books takes place in the fall and illustrator John Sandford shares the glorious colors of autumn in his pictures. Enjoy these Amish treats on a cool, crisp fall day. *(pm, in)*

Shoofly pie

- 1 cup molasses
- 1½ cups hot water
- 1 teaspoon baking soda
- 3 cups flour
- 1 cup brown sugar, well packed
- 1 teaspoon baking powder
- ½ cup shortening
- 2 8-inch pie crusts

Blend molasses, water and baking soda together. In a separate bowl mix flour, sugar, and baking powder. Cut in shortening until mixture is crumbly. Alternate wet ingredient mixture and dry ingredients into pie crusts. Bake 30 to 40 minutes at 350°.

More recipes for this book on pages 4 and 66.

Little Jack Horner

Traditional Mother Goose

Little Jack Horner sat in a corner
Eating his Christmas pie.
He put in his thumb and pulled out a plum
And said, "What a good boy am I!"

Jack's Christmas Pie

- ½ cup brown sugar
- ½ cup flour
- 1 teaspoon cinnamon
- ¼ teaspoon allspice
- 4 cups fresh plums, sliced
- 2 tablespoons lemon juice
- 2 tablespoons margarine
- 2 9-inch pie crusts

Combine sugar, flour and spices. Add plums and lemon juice; mix well. Put this mixture into pie crust and top with margarine. Put top pie crust over all and seal with fork tines. Cut slits in pie crust. Bake at 425° for 30 minutes, or until juice bubbles through slits and the top is golden brown.

The Adventures of Simple Simon

Retold and Illustrated by Chris Conover
Farrar, Straus, & Giroux, 1987

The long version of the traditional Mother Goose rhyme "Simple Simon" is beautifully illustrated in this picture book. You'll have fun finding other Mother Goose characters appearing in the pictures. *(all ages)*

Simple Simon Pie

For each child you will need:

- 1 graham cracker square
- 1 tablespoon butter or margarine
- ½ teaspoon sugar
- 1 Ziploc plastic bag
- 1 foil cupcake liner
- 1 tablespoon cherry pie filling
- 1 tablespoon whipped cream

Place graham cracker, butter, and sugar in Ziploc bag. Let children crush and mix the ingredients together. Press mixture into foil cupcake liner. Top with cherry pie filling and whipped cream.

Nobody Stole the Pie

Sonia Levitin • Illustrated by Fernando Krahn
Harcourt Brace Jovanovich, 1980

In the center of town is a lollyberry tree, and from the berries, the townspeople make a giant lollyberry pie. As the people and animals in town try small samples, little by little the pie grows smaller, until one day it has been eaten up. A town meeting is called to find the thief, but it's soon discovered that no one person has taken the pie—everyone helped to make it disappear. Can't find lollyberries? Substitute cherries! *(all ages)*

Lollyberry Pie

- 2 large pkgs. cream cheese
- 1 cup powdered sugar
- 16-oz. frozen non-dairy whipped topping
- 1 graham cracker crust
- 1 large can cherry pie filling

Mix together cream cheese, sugar, and whipped topping. Put this mixture into graham cracker crust. Top with cherry pie filling. Chill.

Over the River and Through the Woods

Lydia Maria Child • Illustrated by Brinton Turkle
Scholastic, 1974

This is a picturebook version of the Thanksgiving song of the same name. If you are really ambitious, you can cook a small turkey or turkey breast to have after sharing this story. Or you might prefer to have some pumpkin pie. *(all ages)*

Individual Pumpkin Pies

Pie crust

For each child you will need:

- 2 graham crackers
- 1 teaspoon brown sugar
- 1 tablespoon corn oil
- 1 plastic sandwich bag
- 1 muffin cup (foil)

Place crackers, sugar, and oil in the plastic bag. Each child crushes the ingredients in the bag, mixing well. Press the crust into the foil muffin cup. Mix the following pie filling to put into the individual crusts:

Pumpkin pie filling

- 2 cans pumpkin
- 1 teaspoon allspice
- 2 teaspoons cinnamon
- two 1 lb. bags mini-marshmallows
- 2 cartons non-dairy whipped topping

Combine all ingredients, except topping, and cook slowly until marshmallows are melted. In a separate bowl, beat topping, then combine with pumpkin mixture. Let each child fill his or her pie crust. Top with extra whipped topping.

Three Little Kittens
Traditional Mother Goose

Three little kittens, they lost their mittens,
And they began to cry,
"Oh Mother dear, we sadly fear
Our mittens we have lost."
"What! Lost your mittens, you naughty kittens!
Then you shall have no pie."
"Meow! Meow! Meow! Meow!
No, you shall have no pie."

Chocolate Cream Pie

- 4 ozs. chocolate chips
- ⅓ cup milk
- 2 tablespoons sugar
- 1 small pkg. cream cheese, softened
- 3½ cups non-dairy whipped topping, thawed
- 1 graham cracker pie crust

Heat chocolate and 2 tablespoons of the milk on low heat. Cream sugar and cream cheese together. Add remaining milk and melted chocolate. Beat until smooth. Fold in whipped topping. Put this mixture into the pie crust and freeze until firm.

I Smell Honey

Andrea Pinkney • Illustrated by Brian Pinkney
Red Wagon Books, Harcourt Brace, 1997

Red beans, catfish, collard greens and sweet potato pie are being made in a young child's kitchen while she helps her mom in this board book for preschoolers. You may want to make the collard greens on page 83 or make the following sweet potato pie. *(ps)*

Sweet Potato Pie

This sweet potato pie works more a pudding than a pie. Try it in a pie crust if you wish, but skipping the crust, makes it an easy "pie" to make in the classroom.

- 2 sweet potatoes
- 2–3 tablespoons honey
- 2 tablespoons butter

- 1 orange
- 1 egg white

Chop the sweet potatoes into pieces and cook in a pan of boiling water until tender, about 8 to 10 minutes. Drain the water. Mash the potatoes with a potato masher. Add honey, butter and the rind and juice of the orange.

Whisk egg white until stiff. Fold into potato mixture. Grease a casserole dish and spoon in "pie." Bake for 50 minutes or until golden brown.

This Is the Way We Eat Our Lunch

Edith Bauer • Illustrated by Steve Bjorkman
See main entry on page 1

Sweet Potato Pie   See sweet potato pie recipe above.

Ice Cream

"Eighteen Flavors" from Where the Sidewalk Ends
Shel Silverstein
Harper and Row, 1974

In this popular book of poetry you will find a poem about an ice cream cone with 18 flavors. You can buy most of the flavors at the grocery store or ice cream shop, but you might want to try making your own. Here are two different recipes for homemade ice cream. You need an ice cream maker for one, and just a freezer for the other. *(all ages)*

Pumpkin Ice Cream

- 1½ cups sugar
- 1 large egg
- 2 cups whipping cream
- 1 cup pumpkin
- ⅛ teaspoon allspice
- 10 lb. bag of ice

- 2 teaspoons cinnamon
- ¼ teaspoon nutmeg
- 1 teaspoon vanilla
- 2 cups half-and-half
- rock salt

Beat sugar and egg together. Add remaining ingredients, except rock salt and ice. Pour into freezer part of the ice cream maker. Alternate ice and rock salt in container that surrounds the freezer. Let the children take turns cranking the ice cream maker until ice cream freezes. Replace ice and rock salt as the ice melts.

Lemon Ice Cream

- 2 cups whipping cream
- 1 cup sugar

- ⅓ cup lemon juice, freshly squeezed
- 1 tablespoon grated lemon peel

Stir together cream and sugar. Add lemon juice and lemon peel. Pour into a small cake pan. Freeze about 4½ hours, or until firm.

From Cow to Ice Cream
Bertram T. Knight
Children's Press, 1997

From Cows to Ice Cream, is a photo essay that explains how ice cream is made. At the end of the book, there are photographs of several types of ice cream treats that are available at the grocery store. Commercially prepared ice cream products: ice cream in a cone, ice cream sundaes, a chocolate-covered ice cream bar, a Good Humor bar, an ice cream sandwich and Dixie Cups. A short paragraph explains the history of each. This is a good companion book to go with *Let's Find Out About Ice Cream*, by Mary Ebeltoft Reid. *(all ages)*

That Bothered Kate

Sally Noll
Greenwillow, 1991

Kate is bothered by her little sister who insists on doing everything that Kate does, including picking peppermint chocolate chip ice cream as her favorite. Kate's mother tells her that her sister needs her, hoping that Kate will not be so bothered by the mimicking sister. This book will be appreciated by all children who have a sibling. *(ps, pm)*

Peppermint Chocolate Chip Ice Cream

Purchase peppermint chocolate chip ice cream from the grocery store or purchase peppermint ice cream and allow each child to count and add 10 to 20 chocolate chips. Mix well and refreeze until ice cream firms back up a bit, or eat right away.

Let's Find Out About Ice Cream

Mary Ebeltoft Reid • Photography by John Williams
Scholastic, 1996

Beautifully illustrated with color photographs, this book takes the reader on a tour of Ben and Jerry's ice cream factory. After reading the book, it's only appropriate to enjoy a bowl of Ben and Jerry's. If you have a Ben and Jerry's ice cream shop in the area, you may want to consider taking a field trip there. Or just bring in some Ben and Jerry's ice cream, available at most grocery stores. *(all ages)*

Ice Cream   If you wish to make your own ice cream, see the recipes on page 104.

Yummers!

James Marshall
Houghton Mifflin, 1973

Emily Pig is on a diet and invites her friend Eugene to go for a walk with her. All this exercise makes Emily hungry. As she walks, she finds excuses to eat—and eat she does! After enjoying this book you might want to serve something as easy as a small dish of peach ice cream, or you may want to set up a do-it-yourself banana split bar. *(ps, pm)*

Banana Split Bar

Each child can bring in an ingredient. Put them into small bowls. Allow each child to create his or her own banana split. You might wish to include:

- 2 gallons of ice cream
- chocolate syrup
- candy sprinkles
- butterscotch sauce
- whipped cream
- chopped nuts
- maraschino cherries
- shredded coconut
- bananas, peeled and sliced lengthwise

 Beverages

Arthur's Christmas Cookies

Lillian Hoban
Harper and Row, 1972

When Arthur tries to make his mother and father some Christmas cookies, they turn out as hard as a rock and very salty. Arthur is disappointed until he realizes he can paint his salt cookies and hang them on the Christmas tree. *(ps, pm)*

Hot Chocolate

While you make the dough ornaments on page 120, enjoy a cup of hot chocolate, as Arthur did. For each child you will need:

- 1 cup milk
- 1 tablespoon pre-sweetened chocolate milk mix
- 1 marshmallow
- 1 candy cane (optional)

Let each child stir up one cup of chocolate milk. Then pour all the cups of milk into a pot and heat until warm. Place a marshmallow in the bottom of the cup before pouring in the hot chocolate. Stir with a candy cane.

Happy Winter

Karen Gunderheimer
Harper and Row, 1982

A little girl, her sister, and their mother celebrate on a cold winter day. They enjoy many activities and several kinds of food including pancakes, orange juice, and tea for breakfast. They also bake a fudge cake and drink hot cocoa. The recipe for the fudge cake is included in *Happy Winter*. The recipe below is for the hot cocoa to drink with the Happy Winter Fudge Cake. *(ps, pm)*

Hot Cocoa

- 8 cups powdered milk
- 1½ cups sugar
- 1 lb. chocolate drink mix
- 8 oz. dry non-dairy creamer

Mix all ingredients together. Store in a gallon-sized airtight container. When you are ready to serve the cocoa, you will need 1 cup boiling water and ¼ cup hot cocoa mix for each child.

Oh, Lewis!
Eve Rice
Macmillan, 1974

Your students will relate to Lewis as he struggles to keep his winter outerwear zipped, tied, and all in place. After a cold romp in the snow, enjoy hot tea and chocolate cake, as Lewis does. *(ps, pm)*

Hot Tea

Make a pot of regular tea, or mix up a batch of spiced tea to sip on a cold winter's day.

- ⅓ cup sugar
- ⅓ cup instant tea
- 1 pkg. lemonade mix
- 1 cup instant orange breakfast drink
- ½ teaspoon allspice
- 1 teaspoon cinnamon

Mix the dry ingredients well. When you are ready to have a cup of tea, add 2 teaspoons of mixture to 1 cup of boiling water.

More ideas for this book on page 98.

Halmoni and the Picnic
Sook Nyul Choi • Illustrated by Karen M. Dugan
Houghton Mifflin, 1993

Yunmi's grandmother, Halmoni, finds it hard to adjust to life in America and Yunmi fears Halmoni will want to return to Korea. When Yunmi's friends invite Halmoni to chaperone the class picnic, Yunmi worries that her grandmother won't fit in. What if her classmates don't accept Halmoni's dress, her accent and the food—*kimbap*—she makes for the picnic? *(all ages)*

Barley Tea

- 2 tablespoon roast barley*
- 3¾ cup water

Put roast barley and water into a pan. Bring to a boil; simmer until the tea is the strength you would like it. Strain before serving.

*Available at Korean and Japanese markets or groceries.

The Tale of Peter Rabbit
Beatrix Potter
See main entry on page 70

Camomile Tea

Peter, too ill to enjoy bread, berries, and milk, is given some camomile tea. You might wish to make a pot and serve it to the class. If this tea isn't available at your supermarket, try a health food store.

Polly Put the Kettle On
Traditional Mother Goose

Polly put the kettle on,
Polly put the kettle on,
Polly put the kettle on,
We'll all have tea.

Sukey take it off again,
Sukey take it off again,
Sukey take it off again,
They've all gone away.

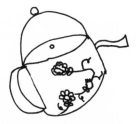

Tea

You'll need 1 tea bag and 1 cup of water per child. Boil the water in a teakettle until it whistles. Pour water into a cup with a tea bag and let the tea steep for about a minute. Provide sugar and cream for those who desire it.

Alice in Wonderland

Lewis Carroll
Scholastic, originally published 1865

Invite your students to a Mad Tea Party based on the one in *Alice in Wonderland*. Use several teapots and fancy teacups rather than disposable cups for this special celebration. Your children might enjoy wearing silly clothes, or wearing their clothes inside out and backwards to add to the madness of the tea party. They might each want to tell a riddle or joke at the party. Wouldn't this be a fun party to invite the mothers and/or fathers to? *(pm, in)*

May I Bring a Friend?

Beatrice Schenk de Regniers • Illustrated by Ben Montresor
Atheneum, 1964 ★ Caldecott Award Book

Each time the king and queen invite a little boy to tea, breakfast, or dinner, he wants to bring a friend. The king and queen always agree for "any friend of our friend is welcome here." But they are always surprised at the unusual types and number of friends that he has. When you have tea with your class, they might want to invite a stuffed animal friend to join you. *(pm)*

Tea

Have a variety of herbal teas available for your students to choose from. Give them the choice of adding honey, lemon, or milk to their tea. Make the tea party special by using a cloth table-cloth and napkins.

Poll Parrot
Traditional Mother Goose

Little Poll Parrot
Sat in his garret,
Eating toast and tea;
A little brown mouse
Jumped into the house
And stole it all away.

Toast and Tea

Bring a toaster to school and let each child make a piece of toast. Have some butter and various jams and jellies on hand that they can spread on their toast. Also, bring 1 tea bag per child and give each one some water just at the boiling point. Steep the tea for about a minute. Have sugar and cream available for those who may want it.

Cider Apples
Sandy Nightingale
Harcourt Brace, 1996

Holly's grandparents worry about their dying apple trees, and Holly learns that without the apple cider money, they will need to sell their cottage. Holly's grandma believes that magic can happen on New Year's Eve, in the moments between the new year and the old. And so Holly finds herself trying to create magic by pouring warm cider over the oldest tree roots in the orchard. Make the cider below, but be sure to save some to drink, too. *(pm)*

Hot Cider with Cinnamon and Honey

- 1 gallon apple cider
- ⅔ cup honey
- 1½ teaspoons cinnamon

Combine ingredients in a sauce pan and boil. Reduce heat and simmer 15 minutes. Serve warm.

Good Lemonade
Illustrated by Marie Zimmerman
Franklin Watts, 1976

If you are going to have a lemonade stand and you want to have more customers than just your brother, you are going to have to serve good lemonade. *(ps, pm)*

Fresh-Squeezed Lemonade

For each child you will need:

- ½ lemon
- 1½–2 cups water
- 2–3 tablespoons sugar

Roll lemons on table before cutting; this makes a juicier lemon. Cut lemon in half and squeeze using a manual or electric juicer. Add water. Stir in sugar to taste. Use lots of ice cubes and enjoy the taste of fresh lemonade!

The Seven Silly Eaters

Mary Ann Hoberman • Illustrated by Marla Frazee
See main entry on page 1

Pink Lemonade

Make the fresh-squeezed lemonade above, adding a bit of maraschino cherry juice to make it pink.

Gregory the Terrible Eater

Mitchell Sharmat • Illustrated by Jose Aruego and Ariane Dewey
See main entry on page 2

Fresh-Squeezed Orange Juice

Instead of using frozen orange juice or cartons of orange juice, you might want to make fresh-squeezed juice with your students. Each child should bring an orange to school. Roll the orange on the table or other hard surface before cutting. This helps to make your orange juicier for squeezing. Each child cuts his or her orange in half, and, using a manual or electric juicer, squeezes the orange for juice. *(ps, pm)*

An Angel for Solomon Singer

Cynthia Rylant • Illustrated by Peter Catalanottl
See main entry on page 26

Grapefruit Juice

Help the children make frozen grapefruit juice, or squeeze some fresh. If you wish to save time, serve ready-made grapefruit juice. *(all ages)*

# Celebrations

Celebrate! in Southeast Asia

Joe Viesti and Diane Hall • Photographs by Joe Viesti
Lothrop, Lee & Shepard, 1996

Colorful photographs illustrate this nonfiction book about Asian celebrations. Among the holidays highlighted is the Moon Cake Festival celebrated in mid-autumn. The festival celebrates the overthrow of the Mongol dynasty in China. According to Chinese legend, rebels hid secret messages inside each moon cake. If possible, shop at an Asian market for authentic moon cakes to share with your children. This recipe is a simplified version. *(pm, in)*

Moon Cakes

- 2 cups sweet (or glutinous) rice*
- ¾ cup coconut cream
- ½ teaspoon sugar
- ½ teaspoon salt
- bananas, raisins, or peanuts for filling

Place sweet rice in cooking pot. Add just enough hot water to cover. Let soak for an hour. After an hour, drain excess water. Mix all other ingredients, except filling, into the rice. Cook over medium heat for about 10 minutes. Stir occasionally. The rice will only be half cooked. Remove from heat and cool. Shape cooled rice mixture into small balls. Poke a hole in the center and put in filling. Reshape ball to cover hole. Traditionally, a secret message is added to moon cakes. This could be added in place of the edible filling. Wrap the balls in foil. Place in steamer and steam for 35 to 40 minutes, until the rice is soft and completely cooked. Cool before opening foil.

*Available at an Oriental market or grocery store.

Lion Dancer

Kate Waters and Madeline Slovenz-Low • Photographs by Martha Cooper
Scholastic, 1990

Lion Dancer is a nonfiction book celebrating the Chinese New Year. Many of the holiday's customs are shared, including the red envelope, fireworks and the traditional dragon. Lotus root is one of the many foods eaten as part of the new year celebration. Other foods mentioned in this book include oysters, fish balls , shrimp, chicken, pork, seaweed and rice. *(all ages)*

Lotus Root

- 2 lotus roots
- 3 tablespoons dark soy sauce
- 1 teaspoon mirin (a sweetened rice wine used in cooking)
- 1 teaspoons sugar
- 1 tablespoon vegetable oil
- salt

Peel lotus root and cut into julienne strips, about 1 to 2 inches long. Heat oil in pan, add lotus root. Cook on high heat, stirring constantly. Add remaining ingredients. Continue stirring and cooking on high for 2 to 3 more minutes. May be eaten hot or at room temperature.

Day of the Dead

Tony Johnston • Illustrated by Jeannette Winter
Harcourt Brace, 1997

An important holiday in Mexico, the Day of the Dead is celebrated for three days starting on October 31. This small, colorful book tells about this holiday where families celebrate the memories of their loved ones by visiting graves, eating festive foods and singing and dancing. This book is a good one to couple with *Pablo Remembers* (see page 7). You may also wish to prepare mole or pan de muertos. You can find recipes for these foods in this cookbook. *(pm, in)*

Empanadas

- 2 cups flour
- ½ teaspoon salt
- 1 teaspoon baking powder
- ½ cup shortening
- ⅓ cup ice water
- vegetable oil
- 1 lb. hamburger or ground pork

Brown meat in a skillet. Season with salt and pepper. Combine dry ingredients. Cut in shortening until mixture resembles fine crumbs. Add water and work into a dough. With a rolling pin, roll on a floured surface. Cut into 2-inch circles with round cookie cutter. Add 1 tablespoon browned meat in center of circle. Fold circle in half and seal by wetting edges and pressing firmly. Heat oil and deep fry empanadas until golden brown.

Oranges and Red Apples

Prepare slices of fresh oranges and apples for your Day of the Dead feast.

More recipes for this book on page 24.

Hooray, a Piñata!

Elisa Kleven
Dutton Children's Books, 1996

Clara, her mother, and her friend Samson go to the market to shop for Clara's birthday party. Clara buys a piñata, a dog she names Lucky, which she quickly befriends, treating it like a real dog. Clara receives another *piñata* for a birthday present. She fills this one with candies for her birthday party celebration. *(all ages)*

Piñata

Buy a *piñata* at a party store, or make one by covering a balloon with papier mâché. Fill it with the same candies that Clara has: almond bars, cinnamon swirls, strawberry rolls, taffy, jelly beans and chocolate kisses. Hang the piñata from a tree branch outside, or a basketball hoop in the gym. Blindfold individual children and allow them to swing at the treat-filled piñata.

La Boda
A Mexican Wedding Celebration
Nancy Van Lann • Illustrated by Andrea Arroyo
Little Brown, 1996

The village of Oazaca is getting ready to celebrate the wedding of Alfonso and Luisa. Music, fireworks, flowers decorating the house, dancing, a parade and festive food are all part of this Zapotec celebration. *Mole* and *higadito* are two of the Mexican dishes that were eaten at this festive event. *(all ages)*

Mole

- ½ cup mole pablano*
- 1½ cups chicken broth
- 1 teaspoon sugar
- 3 lbs. chicken, cubed

In a pan, stir in mole, chicken broth and sugar. Stir and heat until well blended. In a separate baking dish, marinate chicken pieces in mole mixture for several hours or overnight. Bake at 325° about an hour or until brown and tender. Baste frequently. Serve with rice.

*Pablano can be found in the Mexican food section of the grocery store.

Let's Go Traveling in Mexico
Robin Rector Krupp
Morrow Junior Books, 1996

The Mexican feathered serpent, Quetzalcoatl, takes the reader on a tour through the seasons in Mexico. Sights, culture and celebrations are described. *(pm, in)*

Tasting Party

Several foods are mentioned such as corn tortillas, turkey, corn, tomatoes, avocado, pumpkin, coconut, chocolate and vanilla.

Have a tasting party and have your children taste each of the food above or see page 25 to make handmade tortillas. Allow children to peel, cut and taste fresh avocados. This is a fruit many children may not be familiar with.

Three Stalks of Corn
Leo Politi
Charles Scribner, 1976

Angelica lives with her grandmother in California in an area called "Barrio de Picoviejo," where there are many people of Mexican descent. Angelica learns about corn and its importance to the Mexican culture. Every bit of the corn is precious, no part is thrown away, not even the husk. Several foods are mentioned and the children even cook at school! A recipe for *buñuelos* follows.

Buñuelos *(also called "the Shepard's Food")*

This is a popular dish serve to at Christmas.

- ½ cup water
- 2 tablespoons brown sugar, packed
- 1 egg, slightly beaten
- 2 cups flour
- ¾ teaspoon baking powder
- ¼ salt
- 1 tablespoon butter
- vegetable oil
- sugar
- cinnamon
- honey

Heat water and brown sugar together in a pan. Stir continually. Bring to boil and heat several more minutes. Cool. Add beaten egg, mixing slightly. Mix remaining dry ingredients together. Add butter until mixture looks like fine crumbs. Add egg and sugar combination until mixture forms a dough. Knead on a floured surface until elastic, about 4 to 5 minutes. Shape dough into a 20-inch roll. Cover with clean towel and leave for about an hour.

Heat about 1 inch of oil in a large pot. Cut dough into 1-inch slices. On a floured surface, flatten dough pieces into 5-inch circles. Fry in hot oil, turning once, until golden brown. Sprinkle with sugar and cinnamon, or serve hot with honey.

More recipes for this book on page 42.

The Village of Round and Square Houses
Ann Grifalconi
Little, Brown, 1986 ★ Caldecott Honor Book

A young African girl tells about her heritage and life as she grows up in the village of Tos. She explains why the women in this village live in round houses and the men live in square ones. The *fou-fou* made in the story is from white cassava root. If you are unable to find cassava root, sweet potatoes, yams or plantain can be substituted. *(all ages)*

Fou-Fou

- 1½ pounds white cassava root
- 2 cups water
- 1½ teaspoon salt

Cut ½-inch-sized slices from each sweet potato. Peel skins off each piece. Combine ingredients in a pan and bring to a boil. Reduce heat, cover pot and cook until potatoes are tender, about 40 minutes. Drain water from pan and place potatoes in a bowl. Using a hand potato masher, allow the children to mash the potatoes. Dip the masher in cold water from time to time to keep the potatoes from sticking. Mash until the mixture has a sticky paste-like consistency. Moisten hands with cold water and roll potato mixture into small balls and serve as they are—or they serve with a stew to dip the *fou-fou* in as is the book.

Kwanzaa

A.P. Porter • Illustrated by Janice Lee Porter
Carolrhoda, 1991

This nonfiction book describes Kwanzaa, the African American holiday that begins on December 26 and lasts for seven days. Foods is an important part of Kwanzaa, so you may wish to prepare some of the African recipes mentioned in *Cook-A-Book*, such as the sweet potato pie (page 103) or peanut butter soup (page 47). Kwanzaa also celebrates the importance of a good harvest and this is represented with a straw mat (*mkeka*) covered with fruits and vegetables (*mazao*). Your class may wish to wash, cut and prepare fresh fruits and vegetables for a treat to share while discussing Kwanzaa. Or you may want to see page 114 for the recipe for *fou-fou*, an African dish from the village of Tos. *(all ages)*

Other books about Kwanzaa that you may wish to share are listed below. These books mention that families eat food during this holiday, but do not mention any specific meals.

My First Kwanzaa Book by Deborah M. Newton Chocolate, Illustrated Cal Massey. Scholastic, 1992.

The Gifts of Kwanzaa by Synthia Saint James. Albert Whitman, 1994.

Possom Magic

Mem Fox • Illustrated by Julie Vivas
Harcourt Brace, 1991

To help Australian children learn about some of the cities and foods of their country, Mem Fox wrote her first book, *Possum Magic*. Hush and her grandmother, Grandma Poss are possums. Grandma Poss can make bush magic of all kinds, but the best magic of all is making Hush invisible! The two of them travel around Australia together visiting the cities, eating lots of different foods, and making Hush become invisible now and then. A map outlining their journey is included. An added note explains the following foods: *(ps, pm)*

Vegamite Sandwich

Vegamite is available in some grocery stores. Like peanut butter, it is spread on bread. Unlike peanut butter, you need just a thin layer on each slice. I have heard that it is an acquired taste and that Americans tend to use too much. If you can find *vegamite* in a store near you, this would be a new tasting adventure for most children.

Pavlova

- 3 egg whites
- 3 tablespoons cold water
- 1 cup sugar
- 1 teaspoon vinegar
- 1 teaspoon vanilla
- 3 tablespoons cornstarch

Beat eggs until stiff. Add water and continue beating. Constantly beating mixture, add sugar. Stir in vinegar, vanilla and cornstarch. Drop by spoonfuls onto waxed paper. Put waxed paper on a greased cookie sheet. Bake for 45 minutes at 300°. Cool and decorate with fresh fruit.

Claude Has a Picnic

Dick Gackenbach

Clarion, 1993

Claude, the dog, helps his neighbors when boredom sets in with their children, when Mr. Gerald has not returned Mr. Porter's hedge clippers, and when Mrs. Shane wants something to kiss and cuddle. When others in the neighborhood have too much food, Claude gets them all together for a picnic, restoring happiness. *(ps, pm)*

Picnic Food

Picnic food includes: hot dogs, corn on the cob and iced tea. If possible, grill hot dogs and sweet corn on a barbecue grill and serve with iced tea. If a grill isn't available, use the stove or hot plate to cook the food and put a checkered picnic tablecloth on the floor for an indoor picnic.

Teddy Bear's Picnic

Jimmy Kennedy • Illustrated by Alexander Day

Green Tiger, 1983

This book beautifully illustrates the song of the same name. Ask your students to invite their teddy bears and bring a sack lunch to school. Take a walk and spread your picnic blankets on the grass to enjoy your lunches. You might also want to play the record that comes with the book before, after, or during your picnic. Oh, and you might also want to go in disguise! *(ps, pm)*

Teddy Bear Picnic

Instead of having sack lunches, your students might wish to take along the food that the teddy bears enjoyed in the book. The illustrations show the bears dining on sweet corn, sandwiches, celery, potato chips, cake and fruit.

Beach Bunny

Jennifer Selby

Harcourt Brace, 1995

Beach Bunny is a colorfully illustrated story about Harold, a young rabbit, and his mother. They enjoy a day at the beach full of swimming, fishing and shelling, Harold and his mother also enjoy a picnic lunch. *(ps, pm)*

Picnic

Pack a lunch like the bunny in *Beach Bunny*. Harold 's lunch included juice, raw carrots, pickled carrots, carrot chips and carrot cupcakes. If possible plan a trip to the beach and have the children pack these foods to take along. As a class project, see how many other foods made of carrots you can come up with. A recipe for a carrot-raisin salad is also included on page 75 of *Cook-A-Book*.

Picnic

Emily Arnold McCully
Harper and Row, 1984

A mouse family goes on a picnic in this wordless book, but the baby mouse gets lost on the way. If you plan to take your class on a similar picnic, be sure you do not lose any classmates! *(ps, pm)*

Picnic

Pack up a picnic basket and a red and white checked tablecloth and take your class on a picnic. You can enjoy some of the same foods that the mouse family did. They include watermelon, sandwiches, milk, cheese, orange juice, baked beans and sausage. Maybe you will be lucky and find some wild raspberries to eat, just like baby mouse did!

What a Good Lunch!

Shigeo Wantanabe • Illustrated by Yasuo Ohotomo
Philomel, 1978

Little bear is learning how to eat properly with humorous results. Your class will enjoy fixing and eating this well-balanced meal. Since there are several courses, convenience foods are suggested. If you wish to make any of these foods using fresh ingredients or from scratch, recipes appear in other areas of this book for all of them. *(ps, pm)*

A Good Lunch

Your lunch should include 2 to 4 cans of cream of chicken soup, bread with butter and strawberry jam, spaghetti and salad. You could have each child bring an item to prepare and put into the salad, including carrots, lettuce, celery, and cucumbers.

Lunch Bunnies

Kathryn Lasky • Illustrated by Marylin Hafner
Little, Brown, 1996

This book allows you to make two different meals. The first one is what the bunny made at home to practice carrying a lunch tray. The second meal is the one he ate in the lunchroom at school. Both have foods that are easy to make without actual recipes. Substitute your favorite Sloppy Joe recipe for the "Sloppy Bens." If possible work with your school's food service program to see if they can plan the second meal to serve in the school cafeteria one day. If they agree, promise to share *Lunch Bunnies* with the whole school in the lunchroom that day. *(ps, pm)*

Lunches

For the first lunch, serve a carton of milk, peanut butter and jelly sandwich and orange. For the second "lunch line" lunch, serve mashed potatoes, green beans, Sloppy Bens and Jell-o.

I Need a Lunch Box

Jeannette Caines • Illustrated by Pat Cummings
HarperCollins, 1988

When Doris gets school supplies and a new lunch box her younger brother wants a lunch box too. But Mommy says no lunch box until younger brother is old enough to start school. He dreams of lunch boxes—one for each day of the week—and he has a lunch box parade. When Doris' first day of school arrives—younger brother gets a surprise!! *(ps, pm)*

Lunch Box Parade

Have the children bring a lunch box to school. Each child will prepare a peanut butter and jelly sandwich. Also make one or all of the following foods available:

- apples
- oranges
- chocolate cake
- cookies
- pies
- doughnuts

If you wish to make the deserts instead of purchasing deserts, see recipes for chocolate cake, cookies, pies and doughnuts included in this cookbook. Before eating your packed lunches, be sure to have the lunch box parade, allowing the children to share any important information about their special lunch boxes.

King Bidgood's in the Bathtub

Audrey Wood • Illustrated by Don Wood
Harcourt Brace Jovanovich, 1985 ★ Caldecott Honor Book

Everyone tries to think of a way to get the king to come out of the tub. But "King Bidgood's in the bathtub and he won't come out!" Will you know what to do? *(all ages)*

Lunch in the Tub

The king has a feast in the tub. Though you might not want to cook up all he has eaten, you may want to serve cookies or lunch in a cardboard bathtub for your students to re-enact this story. Teachers might want to send home a note suggesting this book and activity for the children to do at home. Maybe mom or dad will serve them lunch in the real bathtub at home!

The Island

Gary Paulsen
Orchard Books, 1988

When Wil Neuton and his family move from Madison, Wisconsin, to the north woods of Wisconsin, he is very disappointed. He cannot understand what the woods have to offer until he discovers the island. Wil decides to camp on the island and makes more discoveries—not only about the island, but also some very important ones about himself and his family. *(in)*

Camp Food

Wil lives on canned food while camping on the island. Set up camp in your classroom, schoolyard, or backyard at home. Serve canned stew, canned beans and fruit cocktail. Just open the cans and eat—no need to heat them if you are going to experience mealtime as Wil does!

Feast for Ten

Cathryn Falwell
Clarion, 1993

Feast for Ten is a counting book that helps young children count from one to ten and then from ten to one, as the family in the book shops for groceries and prepares a meal. *(ps, pm)*

Feast for Ten

Have the children enjoy any or all of the foods prepared in the book. They include:

- pumpkin pie from scratch
- fried chicken
- lima beans (frozen)
- pinto beans (canned)
- jelly beans (bag)

- wax beans, green beans (fresh)
- collard greens
- dill pickles
- tomatoes
- potatoes

A recipe for collard greens can be found on page 83 and pumpkin pie can be found on page 102. The beans do not require recipes as they are heated and served as they come. You may want to eat each type of bean: lima, pinto, jelly, wax and green, and make a graph indicating each child's favorite. Any guess which one of the five will probably come out on top?

The First Thanksgiving

Joan Anderson • Photographs by George Ancona
Clarion, 1984

The reenactment of the first Thanksgiving feast is accurately depicted in this nonfiction book about a truly American holiday. Photographer George Ancona took pictures at Plimouth Plantation, a living history museum, to capture the feeling of the festivities described in the text. *(pm, in)*

Venison

Roast venison at 350° about 35 minutes per pound. Make a gravy and serve with the other traditional food listed for an early Thanksgiving feast.

Turkey Pox

Laurie Halse Anderson • Illustrated by Dorothy Donohue
See main entry on page 68

After reading this book, prepare a turkey dinner with the foods listed below. Be sure to put cherries all over the turkey just as Nana did. Recipes for sweet potatoes, muffins, apple salad and pumpkin pie can be found in Cook-A-Book. A turkey breast or small turkey could be roasted at school or brought in to serve. If making a whole dinner is not feasible, choose just one or two of the foods. (ps, pm)

Turkey Dinner and All the Trimmings

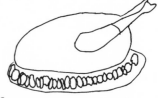

- roast turkey
- sweet potatoes
- mashed potatoes
- brussel sprouts with walnuts
- carrot sticks, celery sticks and olives
- apple salad
- cranberry sauce
- muffins and croissants
- pumpkin, mincemeat and pecan pies

Arthur's Christmas Cookies

Lillian Hoban
Harper and Row, 1972

When Arthur tries to make his mother and father some Christmas cookies, they turn out as hard as a rock and very salty. Arthur is disappointed until he realizes he can paint his salt cookies and hang them on the Christmas tree. Your students can make salt dough ornaments for holiday giving. They aren't edible, but they are pretty—and fun! (ps, pm)

Salt Dough "Cookies"

- 4 cups flour
- 1 cup salt
- 1½ cups water

Mix flour and salt together. Slowly add water until dough is firm but pliable. You might not need to use the full cup and a half of water. Knead dough on a floured cutting board for 8 to 10 minutes, until smooth.

This dough can be shaped by hand like clay, or rolled and cut with cookie cutters. To make cookies like Arthur's, use star, angel, reindeer, and bell-shaped cookie cutters. Poke a hole at the top large enough to thread a ribbon through. Bake at 350° for an hour or more, depending on the thickness of the dough. This dough can be painted or left natural. (Do anything you want with it except eat it!) Store finished ornaments in a dry area. Store unbaked dough in an airtight container in the refrigerator.

More recipes for this book on page 106.

Today Is Monday
Traditional Song • Illustrated by Eric Carle
Philomel, 1993

This text is derived from the words of the traditional song "Today is Monday." The illustrations are lavishly done by Eric Carle. After reading the book and singing the song, share one or more of the following items in class: *(all ages)*

- string beans
- "zooooop"
- fresh fish
- ice cream
- spaghetti
- roast beef
- chicken

If you make string beans allow the children to snap fresh string beans and steam them in a vegetable steamer. Or you can put them into a casserole dish with a small amount of water and cook on high in the microwave 5 to 7 minutes or until tender but still firm.

It's Pumpkin Time!
Zoe Hall • Illustrated by Shari Halpern
Scholastic, 1994

Bold, colorful illustrations and a simple text explain the life cycle of a pumpkin from seed to jack-o'-lantern. Even the endpapers, check both front and back, show how pumpkins grow. Be sure to share this book during the Halloween or fall season. *(ps, pm)*

Pumpkin Seeds

- 2 cups pumpkin seeds
- 1–2 tablespoons vegetable oil
- salt, to taste.

Combine the ingredients above. Mix well. Spread seeds on a cookie sheet. Bake at 250° for 30 to 40 minutes, until crisp. Stir occasionally to brown evenly.

Popcorn
Frank Asch
Parents' Press, 1979

When Sam's parents go to a Halloween party, Sam invites some friends over for his own party. Every friend that arrives brings popcorn. Sam and his friends decide to pop all the popcorn in one pot and before they know it there is popcorn to the rooftop! When Sam's parents come home, they bring a surprise for Sam—more popcorn! Though you will probably not want to pop a full pound of popcorn, you will need to make a lot. *(ps, pm)*

Popcorn

For an experience much like the book and one your children will never forget, place a sheet in the center of the room and put a popcorn popper in the middle of the sheet. Making sure your children are standing back from the sheet, pop your popcorn without a lid on your popper. Though the popcorn will probably not fill the school to the roof, it will pop all over the room.

Let your students enjoy the popcorn that landed on the clean sheet. You might want to do this at your next Halloween party!

The Popcorn Book

Tomie dePaola
Scholastic, 1978

This book gives some interesting facts about America's favorite snack food. Did you know that colonists even ate popcorn for breakfast? They ate popcorn with cream much like we eat cereal. After reading this book with your class, why not try a bowl of popcorn with cream or milk? *(all ages)*

Popcorn with Cream

Pop your popcorn in a popcorn popper, or in a pan on the stove. If you can, make popcorn in a fireplace or build a campfire and make popcorn using a fireplace popper. If you have access to a microwave, you might want to compare making popcorn this way with the ways that the corn is popped in the book. Included in the book are two additional ways to pop corn that you might also want to choose.

Whichever way you choose to pop it, provide bowls, milk, and maybe a little sugar and try eating your popcorn like the colonists liked to eat it!

The Seasons of Arnold's Apple Tree

Gail Gibbons
Holiday House, 1984

Arnold has a secret place under an apple tree. He watches it change through the seasons. In the fall he gathers the apples and makes apple pie and apple cider. Recipes for both of these are included in the book. In the winter he strings popcorn and berries to hang on the tree branches to feed the birds. *(all ages)*

Popcorn and Berries

Pop popcorn the day before you want to string it. It is much easier to string day-old popcorn than freshly popped. Using a needle and long thread, string the popcorn and berries. Hang from a tree near your windows and see how many birds come to feast. If you do this, please continue to feed the birds throughout the winter, as they will become dependent on your feedings.

Title/Author Index